THE FIRST ADVENT

LLOYD STANCLIFF

ISBN: 9798853715578
Reprinted 2013

CHAPTER 1

Jerusalem was a conquered city. There were few to pity the captured vanquished. The city was old, even by the standards of the time. It had seen armies come and go, the great and the small, leaving behind ashes, crumbled walls, and the dead. In an almost hurried fashion, the Israelites, who were stiff-necked people, rebuilt anew on top of the old. No one ever knew how many cities were buried in the countless layers of strata, for their scribes and scrolls were also contained therein.

Rome had been a cruel taskmaster. Its edicts governed daily life and all commerce, ever demanding impeccable obedience. As was custom, procurators were assigned. Pontius Pilate had been placed over Judea, Samaria, and Idumea. Herod Antipas, the second son of Herod the Great, was the tetrarch of Galilee and Perea. It was his father who, by Roman decree, had received the title of King of the Jews and had rebuilt the Jewish temple to increase his popularity.

Distant sounds of the shofar summoning ancient tribes of their ancestors to assemble were still discernible to seasoned ears. The shofar's sound served as a sad reminder of the loss of King David and Solomon and their days of glory. It became the custom for people to rend their garments each day upon awakening to display their anguish. Prayer and devotion became their habit while they longed for prophecy to be fulfilled as if it were their final hope.

They cried for a Deliverer, the Anointed One of Jehovah, God of their ancestors, to redeem them from the hands of their oppressors and never again to be left alone outside His grace or to bend beneath the yoke of their enemies, never again to find barrenness at the holy mountain or to hunger from a beggar's portion of bread.

There was scarcity among their herds of cattle and within their tribes. Disunited and in disarray, each man became his brother's enemy as they struggled to survive. Their faces were hollowed, and their bodies were made of straw, all offering assurance to even the meekest travelers they had come upon easy prey.

Daily life had become ritualized. Their variety was patterned by season, and Roman edict weighed heavily on their outlook. It was good for the old to watch children in endless play, even if it was a reminder of the passing of their blissful ignorance. Teaching their young was mainly composed of lessons about whom to approach and whom to fear. The teaching of the promises made to their patriarchs was always considered foremost in learning and even more so in times of strife.

It took a war to defeat their sons and an invasion to depress their spirits, yet the Jews were accustomed to war and foreign invaders. For whatever recompense, they relished the knowledge that the edicts and intimidation of foreign armies were as transient as the seasons but, regrettably, almost as dependable.

Palestine had always done its share of world trade. Its harbors of Joppa and Ashdod teemed with flurried hysteria as traders from Greece, Rome, and Egypt attempted to outperform one another in the face of waiting merchants. During the heavy trading season, harbors became overcrowded with assorted, multi-shaped ships, all balancing giant masts seemingly without effort. Their canvases hung lifeless, having been exhausted by overly playful winds. Once unloaded, the cargo was routed to favored Jerusalem, Arimathea, and Jericho, serving wealthy families of importance, those placed in stations of authority, and any fledgling marketplace showing promise.

There was an oasis just outside Jerusalem's walls. Shaded by olive and palm trees, it drew travelers on their way to temple worship to drink of its coldness and to rest in its shade. Colorful tents spotted the landscape; their silken tapestries romanticized the wind by caressing a baby breeze. Melodious prayers were already audible from the devout. The wind carried the sound in all directions, making it appear like the desert was chanting.

Come evening, rain was falling in the city; distant thunder clapped and growled like an approaching hungry beast emerging from a century of sleep. One could forgive stars for not guiding the way and absolve those who take them to shelter at first sight of rain, yet one could never pardon the stain of darkness that comes to lose a nation or even a single soul in the great expanse of night.

CHAPTER 2

A man stood silhouetted in a building's portico, safe from the rain, leaning against a wall as if trying to support a burden. His hair was long, resting on his shoulders. He wore a beard as was the custom of Jews; his clothing indicated he was someone from the poorer outskirts of the city, and because of the rain, his clothes clung tightly to him. He did not appear to be in a hurry, nor did it seem as if he were waiting upon anyone's arrival. Had he stood there for a week and a day, it would be doubtful anyone would have stopped to speak to him. Darkness had advanced, securing the streets for itself and one lone figure.

He belonged to obscurity, one of no attractiveness or favor. People would readily turn their heads away. He was despised and rejected by those who knew him, a man of sorrows and a man familiar with suffering. His shoulders slumped like a man heavily laden. His face was drawn, which made him appear older than he was.

An elderly man appeared down the empty street. He maneuvered through the pelting rain, making his way beneath a bundle of wrappings. His size and slow gait gave away his age and strength. Entering a doorway, he disappeared in an explosion of light.

The lone figure began to stir. Without seeing the elderly man's face, he knew it was the rabbi he had sought for counsel. Nervousness swelled within him as he clutched his scroll-filled satchel. Not that he was prone to carrying scrolls, but tonight had become special. On this day, he had finalized a decision that would change him for the rest of his life. The larger part of his maturing had been spent in simplified obscurity, a life meaning little to those around him and not much more to himself. He ventured from his safe covering and sprinted across a muddied street. Pausing to gain strength, he reminded himself of his determination. A knock brought the rabbi to greet him.

There was gentle kindness about the elderly man that helped maintain him in rabbinical circles and popularity with worshipers. His beard and sidelocks, worn only by the most orthodox, were a matching gray. When he spoke, anyone would instantly wonder where the sound was coming from, as his mouth was covered with hair.

"Come in; welcome to my home." He opened the door wide when he saw who it was.

"I waited, knowing you would be delayed in the rain. Is it right for me to come?"

"Yes, of course; come sit by the fire, and I will have a different excuse to warm myself than being reminded of my age. I will pour some wine for your insides and mine as well. I've also discovered it knows what to do with aches and pains." The wine flask was within easy reach. He quickly poured two portions. "Well, now, you spoke about a problem you were having." He sat down, handing him a goblet. "Tell me, how can I help you?"

"I am Jesus of Nazareth. My brothers are James, Joseph, Simon, and Judas. I'm sure you have seen them as well as my sisters."

"Yes, I believe so, and you work as a carpenter."

"Yes, I do."

"Is there a problem with your family then?"

"No, rabbi, they are fine." He became uncomfortable in his chair. "It is my sleepless nights that bring me here. I seek rest for my soul and troubled mind."

"What trouble is this, my son?" The rabbi leaned forward in concern.

"I want to make myself right with God. I want to be in His favor, to do what pleases Him."

"Yes, that is good."

"I have to learn the ways of God. I want Him to be proud of me and enable me to fulfill my destiny."

"Yes, I see. It's good you think that way."

"My mother would tell me stories of how anointed I was."

"Yes, such is understandable; all mothers love their children."

"No, rabbi, what I mean to say is I was chosen by God."

"What do you mean you were chosen?"

"As a child, my mother would tell me stories of her dreams regarding my birth. She always believed she would give birth to one who would become adopted by God to be the Anointed One of Israel."

"You mean the Messiah?"

"Yes, the Messiah, the Anointed of God."

"You mean you were this child?"

Jesus looked straight at him. "Yes, it was me."

The rabbi hesitated and rested his goblet on a nearby table.

"You mean to say you claim to be the Messiah?"

"Yes, as I have told you, as my mother had told me."

"My son, you appear to have let your imagination run wild. Can you not see the magnitude of what you are claiming? Why, when the Messiah comes, he will defeat our enemies and restore the throne of David. Are you prepared to do that?"

"I'm not sure." He looked into himself for the answer.

"My son." The rabbi went out of his way to be as gentle as possible. "How could anybody claim the right to be the Anointed One and not know how to do the mighty deeds expected of such a person?"

Jesus had no answer and stared at the floor.

"You say this because your mother has told you so? Don't you know all mothers are prone to have beautiful stories of their children? Sometimes I think that is a mother's duty. I listen to them all the time."

"Yes, that is true, I suppose. Not only because of what she told me but because of my intuition and the suspicions I have been having."

"Suspicions? What do you mean?"

"I'll admit I have not lived as one would expect the Messiah would. The older I get, the more troubled I become. I have arrived at the point where my conscience keeps me from eating and sleeping; it has taken all my peace and holds me in reproach. I do not blame you for not believing, as I did not believe at first. As a child, I think I did. I was ready to believe anything my mother told me, as what child does not want to please his mother? Yes, as a child, I did believe her stories. Though, as I grew and began to think for myself, I had little patience with my mother and her stories of how blessed and watched over I was. The suffering of my days reflected someone who was accursed rather than one chosen for messianic leadership. I can truthfully say I did not believe such motherly fantasies. Nor did I live my life, wretched existence that it is, as one who is to be a king. Surely, my brothers and sisters never believed in those stories. They certainly never treated me any differently, nor did anyone around me. They despised me for no reason. Their abuse was one of the many reasons I became bitter and resentful."

"Now you feel differently?"

"Yes, I do. I have come to a change in my life where my mind has opened to what is happening around me. I have begun to read the words of the prophets daily, and my awareness has heightened in suspecting what God wants me to do for Him. It has made me feel I have failed in serving the Lord, which I have, for the misery of life had turned me away from God and into sinful living. Though now, I have changed my ways."

"Words of the prophets, you say?" Seeing his eagerness, the rabbi let him empty himself of words.

Jesus reached into his pouch to withdraw a handful of scrolls. "I will show you where it speaks of me. In the writing of 2nd Samuel, when God spoke to David through the prophet Nathan, 'When your days are complete and you lie down with your fathers, I will raise up your descendant after you, who will come forth from you, and I will establish his kingdom. He shall build a house for My name, and I will establish the throne of his kingdom forever. I will be a father to him and he will be a son to Me; when he commits iniquity, I will correct him with the rod of men and the strokes of the sons of men, but My lovingkindness shall not depart from him, as I took it away from Saul, whom I removed from before you. Your house and your kingdom shall endure before Me forever; your throne shall be established forever.'"

He handed the scroll over to the rabbi who, out of politeness, took a moment to glance at it.

"You say you are this person, do you?"

"Yes, I have come to see that now."

"You have become confused. This prophecy has already been fulfilled, for it speaks of Solomon's greatness. Do you see how your imagination has overtaken you? Just because you've begun to read the prophecies does not mean you understand them. It takes rabbis years of study before they understand the prophets' writings. Furthermore, you have not built a temple for the Lord, as Herod, may he rot forever in his grave, has built one for us; even more so, you have no kingdom. You see how strange it is for you to claim to be a Messiah?"

"I realize it is difficult to understand since it took me a while to comprehend these revelations. However, when Herod's temple is destroyed ..."

"When Herod's temple is destroyed?" The rabbi interrupted. "It took them years to build the temple, designed with the best construction. I can assure you nothing will ever happen to it."

"I am convinced it will end in ruin as Solomon's temple did. Then my brother shall rebuild a house for God, and I shall establish a spiritual house that will endure forever. I know many people believe Solomon has already fulfilled that prophecy. If that be so, I ask you, where is the throne of Solomon? For it is written, 'his throne and his kingdom will endure before me forever.'"

"The Messiah will simply rebuild the throne of Solomon."

"Then you are saying it will be rebuilt. In other words, it was a throne that did not endure. If so, then the Scripture does not pertain to Solomon."

The rabbi had no answer. Convinced he would not change Jesus' mind, he allowed him to continue speaking.

"I am driven with concern for the barren, the sick, and the elderly. They are the ones I seek to help."

"You still have yet to become a ruler. How do you propose to make such an accomplishment?"

"I know when the time is right, I will be told how."

"Right now, you do not even know?"

"No, I do not. That was one of the mysteries I hoped you could explain."

"You would like me to explain how to become the Messiah? I am afraid what you are asking is impossible. I am a wise old man and have seen and heard much in my life, so I assure you I know what I'm saying in telling you these are difficult times for Israel. In difficult times, there will always be some overzealous young men who may have all the sincerity and good intentions in the world yet have let themselves go astray in their thinking. What you are going through does not surprise me, for several individuals share your fantasy of delivering our people from the Romans.

"Now listen to me. I was hoping you could think about what I've told you and be rational. There's no shame in admitting you've overreacted to whatever circumstances made you this way. There is no shame at all."

"But I ..."

"No, now listen. If I had a blessing for every person I spoke to who claimed to be the Messiah, I would be the richest man in the city." He smiled, rising to his feet. "The only way I can help you is to caution you to rethink what you have learned in the Scriptures with a more practical mind. Then I am sure you will see these matters clearly. Go to the temple and ask for the Lord's guidance. If you are sincere, He will help you. Take a sacrifice with you for atonement to have peace in your soul.

"Now come, the rain has stopped, and I know you have a long walk home before you." Jesus stood while stuffing away his scrolls and was escorted to the door. "Think about what I have said; you will realize how the idealism in you young people can sometimes play tricks on your mind."

"I will do as you say, rabbi. I will go to the temple, but I know the answers I shall get will be the same. I will hear the voice I hear now, the voice of my conscience. Truthfully, I can only live by my conscience."

The rabbi opened the door, bidding farewell. "I've enjoyed our talk, Jesus." He patted him on the back. "We will talk some more another time if you like. I am glad you felt confident enough to confide in me. It shows I am not useless as some people think." He laughed, holding open the door.

"Goodbye, rabbi, and thank you for your ear."

"Good night to you."

He closed the door, leaving Jesus in the lonely dark of night. He walked through the water-soaked streets, heading for his home. While he did not get what he came for, it was still beneficial for him to speak his mind and openly confront another with the burdens of his heart. Never had he been so bold as to claim a ministry that an average person would mightily ridicule and scoff.

The air was cold and damp, yet many returned to fill the streets. Life had again appeared in the city with its flurry of night travelers, pickpockets, and Roman soldiers. Jesus walked casually through the maze of familiar and not-so-familiar faces. The better part of him was immersed in thought, half of him grateful to have finally spoken his mind to someone and the other half plagued with fearful possibilities that he had just made a grandiose fool of himself. He knew the old rabbi would not betray him, which offered some comfort.

It is difficult for a person to change his life, giving up the secure and familiar for a vague outline of a future well filled with insecurities, yet that was the quest he was professing. He discovered that such a decision can make one feel completely alone. He was driven by whatever haunts a person to change the temperament of his being, a man laden with remorse as one is when he discovers he had made a wrong turn in life somewhere in the past.

He crossed the market arcade, still fuming with the smell of vegetables, now governed by mice that seemed to be doing their browsing. Working as a carpenter, he had swelled his hands; his shoulders were broad and muscular. It availed him a living as long as tastes were kept simple, and it provided enough activity to keep his mind off daily survival. There were few noteworthy events for remembrance's sake and very little in the future to cause him to look forward.

Derelicts and the homeless came out of their makeshift shelters to continue with what was left of the evening's begging. They instinctively put their hands out and moaned as he went by them, conditioned by years of loyal dedication to the art. One could easily have called this Jesus a loner and would have done so, having been in his company for a moment, for powers and causes unseen had produced an introvert. Like most of his kind, he found joy in contemplating the mysteries of life, experiencing the manifestation of total fulfillment when he believed he was near to solving life's riddles.

Water still dripped from building roofs, darkening whatever it touched, resounding in street puddles. Jesus approached a well-lit area filled with taverns and joyful discourse from their patrons. Noise from their instruments made for a dancing, festive mood. Music is usually heard in this quarter, and those patronizing it find something to celebrate almost every night. It was an area where it was understood one should never walk alone. Prostitutes prowled their habitats while the more unscrupulous lay waiting in dark alleys for someone to show a sign of weakness.

A man from the neighborhood who saw Jesus from across the way hurried toward him to gain his attention.

"Jesus, where have you been? I've been looking all over."

"I have been busy," Jesus said, recognizing him instantly. "Why do you seek me?"

"Look at what I've got." He emptied his purse of gold and silver coins into Jesus' hands.

"Where did you get it?" Jesus felt its weight.

"From the timber merchant who came to Jerusalem with his caravan. I started one of his tents on fire just outside the city where they were camped. When they ran to it, I went into the main tent.

It did not take long to find. Pretty good, huh? Come, my friend, and help me celebrate. We will drink and eat the night through and greet the sunrise. We will spend the evening in wine, song, and dance." He returned the coins to his purse.

"No, I don't want to go with you."

"Why? Aren't you feeling well?"

"No, I'm not sick. I would just rather not."

Jesus turned from him and walked away, passing crisscross among the city's outcasts. His friend shrugged his shoulders and scurried away in the opposite direction.

CHAPTER 3

A few weeks later, a man called John came out of the desert of Judea. One who lived on locusts and wild honey; he too, was a Jew and wore a wrapping of animal skins around him. His voice thundered before the people as he preached the baptism of repentance for the forgiveness of sins. He began baptizing people in the waters of the Jordan River. Such a respected and revered man was he that the entire countryside of Judea, and those who dwelled in Jerusalem, came confessing their sins and waited their turn to be baptized by him.

The Jews of Jerusalem sent priests and Levites to John asking for his identity, for the crowds were of great numbers.

They asked, "Tell us why you have come?"

Knowing what was on their minds, John answered, "I am not the Christ."

"What then?" they asked. "Are you Elijah?"

He answered, "No, I am not Elijah."

"Are you the prophet?"

He denied it, saying, "Nor am I the prophet."

In seeking an answer to report back to those who sent them, they asked, "Make a claim about who you are, so we will not go away unsatisfied."

John answered, "I am a messenger sent to prepare the way."

They traveled back to Jerusalem to inform their superiors.

Each day thereafter, John stood atop a hill to address the crowds of newcomers. "Repent while you may, for the day of the Lord is upon you. There is one coming after me whose sandals I am not fit to touch. I baptize you with water, yet he will baptize you with a holy spirit and fire. A winnowing fork will be placed in his hand so that he may thoroughly clean his threshing floor. Then he will gather his wheat into a barn and burn the chaff with unquenchable fire. The ax is already laid at the tree's root; every tree bearing good fruit will be saved, but those that do not will be cut down and thrown into a fire."

Then came members of the Pharisees and Sadducees, bringing with them their hypocrisy, wanting baptism by him. John was angry when he saw them coming. He shouted, "You brood of vipers, who warned you to flee from the coming wrath? Go and return with an extra offering of fruit and food in proportion to your repentance. Nor should you believe the promises of God are assured because you are sons of Abraham; for know well, God can raise sons for Abraham from these stones."

A few days later, the man, Jesus, came from Nazareth in Galilee to the Jordan River. Entering the water, he approached John, saying, "Baptize me, John."

Taken aback at his presence among sinners confessing themselves, John said, "You want me to baptize you? Why, you should baptize me!"

Jesus said, "Let it be so to fulfill all righteousness." He lowered his head in shame and gave no indication he would speak further. In the presence of onlookers, John baptized Jesus in the waters of the Jordan River and said nothing else to him.

Jesus walked from the water, quiet and contemplative. When he reached the shore, he wiped the water from his face. John stood motionless, waist-deep in the river, and observed him leaving. While watching, John had a vision of the heavens opening and saw the power of the Lord descend on Jesus in the form of a dove. It was from that day Jesus' ministry began; from that day, he lived according to the lawful precepts of his ancestors.

He was first moved to return to Nazareth but felt compelled to sojourn in the desert. There he was to remain for fasting and prayer. He came upon a man camping in the wilderness. As Jesus walked by, the stranger said, "You think you are the Son of God all of a sudden? Well, there is an easy way to find out. If you are God's adopted Son, turn these stones into bread."

Jesus stopped and answered, "Man shall not live on bread alone, but on every word that proceeds out of the mouth of God." He began walking, leaving the desert man behind.

"Is that the only excuse you can think of presenting? If you can't do it, why not just say so?" The man yelled after him. "If God adopted you, you surely could do it! Do you hear me? If you were the Anointed One, you would have more than a piece of desert around you! Wouldn't you?" The man shouted when Jesus refused to turn around. "Well, wouldn't you? You're only fooling yourself! Do you hear me? You're only fooling yourself!"

Jesus remained alone in the desert, determined not to leave until he had received answers to all the questions plaguing his soul. The land was barren and dry; the heat made him suffer to exhaustion. From there, he carried himself to the coolness of a mountaintop. The same man appeared as if he had been waiting for him.

"If you are the adopted Son of God, throw yourself down from here; for it is written, 'He will give His angels charge concerning you; in their hands, they shall bear you up, lest you may strike your foot against a stone.'"

Jesus moved away from the edge, for he was afraid, and said, "It is also written, 'You shall not tempt the Lord your God.'" He began to move away from the desert man.

Again the man yelled after him, almost having to give chase, but Jesus would still not turn around. "Is that your only excuse? What are you afraid of happening? Go ahead, throw yourself down; see if you should hit a stone. If you were the adopted Son of God, you would be able to do it! Well, wouldn't you? You're only fooling yourself!"

Lastly, when he saw Jesus hurriedly leaving, he ran up to him, saying, "Whereas I have perceived you to be a proud man, I know someone who will give you all those cities you can see in the distance and all their glory if only you would worship him."

Jesus turned and answered, "No longer will I serve him. You shall worship the Lord your God, and Him only shall you worship."

Continuing, Jesus left the man behind and returned home to Nazareth.

CHAPTER 4

It was a day made clear by the wind in which the bustle of daily life was carried on by merchants and artisans alike. A man made his way around the carts and workers, passing into the gate of Jesus' home. His beard was long and untrimmed in compliance with Hebrew law; his hair rested on his shoulders as if the wind had blown it there. On the surface, nothing about him made him seem out of the ordinary. The whitewashed stucco walls of the home glistened and bulged out in round clumps from years of repair and mending. He was drawn by the sounds of activity in the shed where three men absorbed in the reshaping of wood did not notice him until he spoke.

"I am looking for one named Jesus." He announced his presence over their hammering. "I was told he lives here."

Only one stood erect, the smallest of the three; his young face brightened with eager alertness at the sight of a visitor.

"Yes, he lives here; he is my brother," he said. He used the opportunity to wipe his brow.

"Is he here now? I wish to speak with him."

The young man paused before answering, his attention caught by the visitor's pouch that hung from his shoulder. "You will find his majesty out back," he said. He couldn't help but laugh at what he just said.

Walking to the building's rear, he found the yard cluttered with planks and scraps of wood orphaned long ago, reflecting grotesque remnants of what they used to be. Jesus was in the far corner, sifting through timber, looking for matching pieces. The visitor stood motionless and breathed relief as one does after seeing someone for whom he has long waited.

"So, you are called Jesus," he said.

"Yes. What do you want of me?" Jesus answered, now moving through the wood more slowly.

"I have waited for you."

"What have I to do with you?" Jesus came around to face him.

"I am a prophet of the Most High God." He opened his shoulder bag, grabbing a handful of scrolls. "Here they are."

Jesus took the scrolls and turned them over in his hands. "I don't understand. What are these?"

"What you are holding is a record of the coming of the Messiah."

"What kind of record is this?"

"It is the story that will be told, what will be recorded, and how your first advent will be presented."

"How could you possibly know about me?"

"This is how I know. The Lord has placed the burden on me to perform this task. Be sure what you are holding was achieved through tribulation I could not describe. As iron is tempered in fire, I have been disciplined to perfect this work for the Lord. I need not tell you I did not volunteer for this work; the choice was not of my accord. If ever I am granted the opportunity, I would pass this task off to the first passer-by I can find, as the Lord is no respecter of persons. Though I am sure you have found that out for yourself.

"At the river, the Lord God pointed you out when John said, 'Behold the Lamb of God who looks away from the world's sins,' and you were repenting for your sins and being baptized by him. I have already spoken to John and given him his tasks; now I am to deliver yours as the will of the Almighty will have it. Now John must decrease, and you increase, for your time has come."

Jesus opened the scrolls and began to read, alarmed at what he saw. "I have never had these achievements, nor can I even conceive of doing them."

"I know, but you shall, for that is your guide. One cannot record all your events or write down all your words, yet the world's people must understand and begin to learn. This is all the heavens care to reveal to the world and how it will be presented. In the end days, at the Lord God's choosing, there shall come another prophet like me to be a mentor for another coming. Right now, let us be concerned with the present. Many of the smaller events have been left out. I will complete the writing as we go."

"You mean you are staying with me?"

"Yes, I will follow along. I will be there if you need me and absent when you do not. I must ensure you do and say what is written so it can be recorded."

"That it can be so recorded," Jesus echoed him as he read, becoming amazed at it all.

"Let me leave those scrolls with you for your study. I will return in a few days. Then we will begin to make it all happen, for the patience of the Lord is about to run out."

"The patience of the Lord is about to run out." Jesus was shocked by it all. "Very well, I will read them."

"What of your brother? Does he know anything?"

"I have four brothers; I know they think I am crazy."

"No matter, I will return to you so we may begin. Goodbye, my friend. I'm glad to have finally met you."

Jesus sat, watching him leave, then turned his attention to the scrolls.

At the insistence of Herodias, the wife of Herod Antipas' brother, Philip, Herod sent his soldiers to arrest John. When John was before the sons of Israel, he publicly defamed her, saying, "She should not lie with her husband's brother." Thus, John was bound and placed in prison. While Herod desired to put him to death, he feared the crowds, for they regarded John as a prophet. Not wanting to incite an uprising, he became content with keeping John from preaching.

By the day the prophet returned, Jesus had read and reread the scrolls several times. He had found them upsetting, yet they gave him strength and encouraged him to reaffirm his belief in himself.

"I did not conceive of the end as being so horrid," Jesus said to him, still fully amazed at it all. "Of course, I thought of being chastised and perhaps even dying, yet it frightens me to see it written so."

The prophet tried to comfort him about what had been written in the scrolls. "No man cares to face death, especially at the hands of the Romans."

Jesus challenged the prophet's writing. "You say I am going to be crucified? How can this be so? In all my imaginings of what God had planned for my life, I had never imagined such a horror. Nor did I have such insight when I turned from my ways and began serving God."

"As I have said, the Lord is no respecter of persons. Nor do I find your blindness surprising, as it is written, 'Who is blind but my Servant?' God had allowed your eyes to be closed to make you a guilt offering so that you would experience all that man had to experience, bear the grief the iniquity of man had caused, and be knowledgeable of his weaknesses and needs. God has used evil for His glory. By allowing the devil to blind your eyes, Satan has caused you to fall prey to the sins defeating mankind, to make manifest to you how fallen creation is from its Creator. God has used the devil to bring you to your inheritance, where you will help bring Satan to defeat. There will also be a time when God will use Satan to stand in your position; this is only another way God will use evil for His good and to demonstrate His glory. What you do not understand, I will teach you."

"How accurate can you be? How do I know you have not made some mistakes? Scriptures can be interpreted in many ways. When I read the prophetic writings, I never saw my name associated with such a punishment as crucifixion."

The prophet then showed him all the prophetic passages referring to his ministry and God's promises for him. It took many days of teaching before Jesus' mind became open to what must pass. In time, he was reconciled to the will of God.

"I pray God will give me strength at the time of my death," Jesus said. "I've failed at everything I've ever done in life. Everything I've ever had has been taken from me in one way or another. Perhaps this is one endeavor I could do right. I do not look forward to suffering the agony of it all."

"I do not know what you did in your life to have deserved such a punishment, yet God is a righteous judge and chastises those He loves."

"It is true; I have been wretched in my days and am weary of carrying the guilt and shame of my wrongful ways. If God has adopted me as His Son and has seen fit to punish me, then I will consent to my fate. Then I shall be glorified as a king, as you have told me, and work the beginning of salvation for the spirit of man."

The prophet tried to encourage him further by quoting, "'When your days are complete, and you lie down with your fathers, I will raise up your descendant after you, who will come forth from you, and I will establish his kingdom. He shall build a house for My name, and I will establish the throne of his kingdom forever.' You are that very person, at least one of them. That is a lot to look forward to having. Of course, it means sacrificing your present life for a greater one of glory and eternal splendor."

"Tell me of the resurrection; will it be as glorious as you have written?"

"Yes, it shall, for you will rise from the dead and never die again."

"Never to die again," Jesus said. These were words he had never used. The magnitude of the realization caused a long period of silence between the two.

The prophet went to Jesus' home one day when no one was there except for Jesus' mother, Mary. She was sweeping out the area and tending to her household chores. She looked up to see him coming and leaned on her broom. Her face and hair were as haggard as her clothing. A permanent grimace had been formed by years of disappointment and despair.

"No one is here. Come tomorrow if you want to buy something." She spoke as if she didn't care if he ever came back.

"I'm not here to buy. I'm looking for Jesus' mother."

"I'm his mother. What do you want of me?"

"Would you mind if I ask you questions about him?"

"What kind of questions? Who are you anyway?"

"I'm a friend of Jesus, and I came to speak to you about him."

"What about him?"

"I'm writing an account about Jesus, and I wanted to ask you if you knew you were the mother of the Messiah?"

"Mother of the Messiah, ha! Is that what he told you?"

"I know you must have been asked that question before."

"I've never been asked such a question. Why should he tell you that? Now he thinks he is the Messiah, huh? All I need is for him to go around committing sacrilege."

"I would think you would be happy to be the mother of the Messiah."

"Do I look happy to you?" She turned away to feed the chickens. "Messiah, indeed. After the way he has lived his life? I must have been crazy to get married and have children in the first place. There must have been a curse on my head to make me get married and have children." She shook her head in disbelief.

"Then you don't believe in Jesus?"

"Do you see any change in the world? Everything is as it always was, and you ask me if I believe in my own son, of all people!"

"Jesus has changed his ways and has turned to obey God."

"Changed, huh? Well, I hope it's for the better. And I'd like to see just how long it lasts."

"I believe he is the Messiah."

"Then you're as crazy as he is."

"Was there ever a time you believed in him?"

"What difference does it make now? All I know is I'm tired of living this miserable life. If I'm not tired, I'm sick; if I'm not sick, I'm tired. And I'm tired of being sick and tired. There may have been a time. I remember when I was a young girl, I dreamed of growing up to be the mother of the Messiah. Then again, all young girls dream of that. When he was a boy, I would pretend he was the Anointed One. I raised him to think he was anointed. Of course, all mothers do the same. I came to see how fruitless all that was. Why are you writing this down?"

"This is for the account of Jesus and his life."

"Why? Who would be interested in such information?"

"Many will be when they see how God is with him."

"I can see you are crazy."

"If you see a change in Jesus and see him performing miracles, would you believe in him then?"

She paused from her chores. "I don't know. I'm afraid to answer that."

"I'd like to talk to you again." He put away his scroll. "You'll be surprised when you see what is to be revealed. I'll say goodbye for now. It is a pleasure to meet you."

She watched him leave the yard and moved to the gate to see where he was going.

CHAPTER 5

On a fair day filled with cool breezes, the prophet and Jesus strolled through a market area in Jerusalem. Multiple trading ships had arrived to unload their cargo. Their arrival caused a flurry in the city. Porters carrying huge crates on their hunched backs followed one another through winding, narrow streets like a tribe of ants burdened with transporting nest material twice their size. The prophet stopped to purchase grapes and, while filling his mouth, reached into his pouch and handed Jesus a scroll.

"Here, take this. Go over amongst that crowd and read it to them."

"What is this?" Jesus asked, opening the scroll.

"Something I wrote last night as the Lord directed me."

"If you already wrote it, why should I have to read to them what you wrote?" He spoke as he was reading.

"It is so I could record you said those words." He spoke with his mouth full of grapes. "If you are asked if you said those teachings, you could truthfully answer you did."

"Very well. If the Lord has directed you, I will. Where should I go?"

"Move over there by all the shoppers; whether they care to listen to you is insignificant at the moment, you still did address them."

"You can be sure they will not pay any attention." Jesus moved toward the crowd.

The prophet held up his grapes and twirled them, looking for a choice pick. "Probably." He clearly wasn't expecting a great response.

The crowded square overflowed with bustling people. A constant roar of bargaining and its expected arguments dominated among merchants and buyers, creating an echo of near confusion. Jesus stood among them; opening the scroll he read aloud, "Behold! The kingdom of Heaven is at hand. Those who have eyes, let them see; those who have ears, let them hear. I come before you to announce your salvation."

He continued to read the passages while being completely ignored. Shoppers bumped into him while trying to get from one merchant to another, oblivious to what he was saying.

Jesus ended yards away from where he initially stood, having been shuffled there by the crowd. When he was done speaking, he wound the scroll and returned to the prophet, who was leaning against a wall, taking in the sights.

"Finished?"

"Yes, I'm finished, and be sure it was a waste of time. As I said, no one would stop and listen."

"Come, let us go." The prophet gathered his scrolls.

They proceeded to surrounding towns and villages and returned to Jerusalem, stopping to speak to people as the prophet would direct. As expected, few cared to listen.

They paused by a well to drink and rest. Seizing the opportunity, Jesus began to ask questions.

"Tell me more of God. What does He expect of me?"

"I tell you, God Himself told me He shall receive your worship and loyalty, regardless of your disbelief, in keeping with His promise given to David by the prophet Nathan. The Lord has given you a thirst to serve Him."

"Why did the Lord God not answer my prayers when the times came for me to ask His help?"

"This I do not know. The Lord works in strange and mysterious ways. Though be sure, as David went on to serve God with diligence after his son was taken as payment for his sins, so must you serve the Lord with as much diligence, even if it means dying on a cross. As David was chosen to lead, you have been chosen to lead. If death is the payment you must make for your sins against Him, then dying on the cross is what you must do, that is, if you want to become a king."

"Yes, yes, I want to be a king. Who would not? I have certainly changed my ways, for I am eager to serve God now. Indeed, I have decided to offer myself as payment for my sins."

"This is good, for it is how the Lord shall have it."

"I keep thinking of the resurrection. To rise from the dead is assured, is it not?"

"Yes, you shall rise."

"I have fears and doubts; maybe I am insane, as my family keeps telling me, for no one has ever returned to life after being crucified."

"What about me? Am I insane as well? You must have faith in God and His word. You must know by now I have no reason to lie to you."

"Yes, of course, you would have no reason to lie. It seems you believe in me more than I do." It was easy to see that Jesus was gaining confidence.

"Look there, here come those imbecile fishermen we met at the shore. You should tell them of your ministry again. See if they would walk with you through the city and teach them to preach of you. It would help if you could show a miracle."

"A miracle, you say! It would help me to see a miracle! How can I make a miracle happen?"

"You don't make miracles happen; they will come from your Father. Have you ever tried asking for something that might glorify His name since you were baptized of water and changed your ways?"

"Why, no, I have not."

"Then I urge you, Son of David, to ask, and you will be well surprised at the outcome. Ask God to heal the sick you come upon. If they were healed, they wouldn't fall away from believing in you. It would be good to have close followers to give testimony. I am sure He will comply if you ask it for His glory. I will follow behind to observe whatever spontaneous reactions you get from people."

"Very well." Jesus rose to greet the fishermen.

"Hello, rabbi," the taller one said. His sarcasm triggered a chuckling among themselves. "What news of God do you have today? I am Simon Peter; this is my brother Andrew, and our friends James and John. You met us on the shore yesterday."

"Yes, I remember. I have plenty of good news," Jesus said. He tried not to look intimidated by them. "Come with me and listen as I go now to tell the people."

They signaled one another to see if all were in agreement for an amusing time. "Sure, we'll go with you, rabbi. Lead the way." So, they followed him.

When they reached a crowded area, Jesus began having second thoughts about being sent out alone. He hesitated from approaching anyone for fear of ridicule. He walked among the people as if he knew where to go and stayed one step in front of his newly acquired acquaintances so that he would not have to listen to their snickering. Peter was the first to make a spectacle of himself. Waving his arms in the air, he attracted attention. "Sons and daughters of Israel, come hear the word of the Lord!" He bellowed as loudly as possible and chuckled to himself. His two friends laughed and then scurried to catch up to Jesus, who was pretending not to have heard them.

Jesus seemed to be waiting for the right moment to speak to anyone, but somehow, that moment kept evading him. Because of the crowd, a man laden with his purchases turned a corner and bumped into them. Peter said, "Hey, watch where you are going! Don't you know who this is?" he said. He nodded toward Jesus. "Why, the rabbi here will call down fire from Heaven on you just like that." He snapped his fingers and looked at Jesus. "Won't you, rabbi?" Again they chuckled, as it seemed anything regarding Jesus was good for a laugh. Jesus kept silent and moved on into the city.

They arrived in the busiest area just in time to join a crowd watching Roman soldiers arrest a group of militant youths. Such a sight always aroused sympathy for captives as their fate was well-known by all. It had become almost a daily expectancy to witness such Roman discipline, which came to be applauded by an array of spitting. When the last of the Roman detachment moved on with their catch, so too did the crowd, dispersing as quickly as it had formed.

Much of Jerusalem was in poverty. The foulness of the city vaporized in the hot sun, permeating through stone walls to become a stench to the nostrils. People hungered for everything one could desire to have. Their Roman oppressors kept them desolate in body, mind, and spirit. Their needs were fathomless, but of all the gifts one could give, the greatest of them would be hope. For there is life in hope, strength, and invincibility, and nourishment for the body and soul. Looking upon their saddened faces, Jesus felt compassion and began to speak on his own, having no need for a mentor. He approached a group of people when he noticed them sitting in quiet despondency.

"My people, the kingdom of Heaven is at hand. Today you thirst and hunger, yet I shall take you beneath my wing, and you shall suffer no more. I am Jesus of Nazareth; I have come to take you into my kingdom. There you shall have everything you need; you shall not thirst nor hunger. I shall bring you into my home, a land of milk and honey. Come if you have no money, for I shall be your king."

Jesus went forward to a crippled child who sat on the ground. "Father, I pray you touch this little one for your glory." He laid his hands on the child's head, and when he did, the child began to rise and walk. When the people saw this, they were amazed, for the child had been born a cripple. They became so occupied with the child that they did not notice Jesus was as surprised as they were. It was the first time he had displayed so much faith.

The crowd came forward and asked, "Who are you that you can do such a miracle?"

He responded to them, feeling comfortable in their acceptance, "I am Jesus of Nazareth; come follow me and learn of my kingdom."

In a short while, he had acquired a large gathering of people astounded at such a bold person who had spoken to them like no other, one who had performed remarkable feats of healing, and they knew God was with him.

He went throughout the city, preaching of the kingdom of God and giving hope to the forlorn. To his surprise and his followers, there were many such miracles found that day. Those blind were able to see. The lame walked, and evil spirits were driven away. Come evening, his newly acquired fishermen friends no longer ridiculed him but treated him with respect and reverence, saying, "Truly this is the Son of God."

Now there was a wedding in Cana of Galilee; the mother of Jesus was there, as was Jesus with some of his followers and his brothers James, Joseph, Simon, Judas, and his sisters. They moved the ceremony outside to accommodate members of both families and their guests. Their dancing and gaiety lasted through-out the afternoon and early evening, with people showing no signs of returning home. Jesus walked across an open area around the dancers and musicians. His sister approached and stopped him.

"Where are you going? Do you plan to talk to those over there? Do me a favor and do not come out with your insane talk tonight, for many of my friends here. I do not care to be embarrassed by you and your sudden holy attitude."

"Leave me be!" Jesus said. He moved away from her. He wasn't about to listen to her nagging and had even less concern for her friends. He went to the table, helping himself to another plate of food.

His sister saw her mother passing with two boys and, becoming alarmed with what she thought he might say, approached her. "Mother, look at Jesus there; he is about to speak to those people. I know he is planning on it, and my friends are here. Is it right I am made into a laughingstock?"

"Jesus? Where is he? I need him." She scanned the room and spotted him across the way. "Why don't you leave your brother alone for a change?" She motioned for the boys to follow her and quickly made her way to him.

She gained his attention. "Jesus, we are out of wine." She turned to the boys and brought them closer to him. "Do as he tells you." Then she returned to sit down.

"What have you there?" Jesus looked into their urns.

"It is water, sir," said a boy.

"Place them on the table and return for them in a few minutes."

Jesus continued to fill his plate while they did as he had instructed. He did not speak to anyone as his sister feared but sat alone and ate, feeling lost as to what to do. His eyes remained fixed on the urns. It was comforting to him to know his mother had acquired such faith in him, yet such a request appeared to be beyond the limitations he had set for himself. He sat pondering how to approach God with such a request of no importance. Knowing other guests had heard her request made him uncomfortable, so he moved away. He bowed his head in prayer, giving the appearance he was offering thanks for the food, and prayed almost apologetically that he was asking for such a miracle.

In a short while, the young boys returned for the urns and took them to the head table, where they poured wine from what was once water. Jesus stood to better his view. He saw the redness of what they were pouring and, going to them, tasted it. The water was indeed wine. Overcome with amazement, he left the crowd to thank God for answering his prayer.

CHAPTER 6

Jesus had just returned from having spent the day preaching of his kingdom. He saw the prophet resting in the shade of a tree but said nothing to him. He walked past him angrily, heading for a well where he dipped his face into a bucket of cool water.

"I went preaching today as you wanted. They spat on me and threw stones." He searched his head for blood. "What sense is there for me to preach as I do? Even if they should believe, which they don't, they will only forget a few days from now."

"No, they won't forget. Trust me; I know what I am talking about."

"The very people I'm preaching to are the same ones I would have smashed in the face a few months ago."

"You have to put away your bitterness and start loving people. You can't keep blaming others for the misery in your life. It was written that you will be made to bear their iniquities. Such is why you have been brought to tolerate the cruel, unloving, and loathsome ways of those around you."

Jesus moved to sit down next to him. "Tell me, why do I have to be chastised in such a manner as crucifixion to receive God's forgiveness? Didn't the baptism of John wash away my sins?"

"John baptized in water for the remission of sins so that men should be humbled, declaring themselves sinners before their brethren and stimulating remorse for their iniquities."

"Then I have been made right before God?"

"Yes, made right so you may receive your ministry. You must also receive death on the cross. Because your station is higher, you must receive a greater punishment, to be punished with 'the rod of men and the strokes of the sons of men.'"

"Why can I not present a goat or lamb to the high priest so that I could be forgiven as the others are? Am I to be worse off because I am anointed by God?"

"The Lord chastises those He loves. God is willing to demonstrate His wrath and to make His power known to you. He has endured your lack of faith with much patience as you prepared yourself for destruction with disbelief. Evidentially, God considers your sins not menial, but mortal. The punishment must fit the crimes.Those He has called to offer more are also called to endure more."

Their attention was taken by an old man who approached, dragging a litter. The weight of it bent his body to near collapse, for he had come a long way.

"Please, sirs," he said to them, "can you tell me where I can find Jesus of Nazareth, who performed the miraculous healings? My son is dying of a lesser illness than many of those healed, and I know he could save my boy."

"I am Jesus of Nazareth," he said, rising to greet him. He looked at the boy, who was extremely pale with sickness. Feeling compassion, Jesus laid hands on him. "Father, if it be your will, raise him from his infirmity for your glory." The boy was immediately healed and returned to his father. The old man wept with rejoicing, for it was his only son. Then the old man and his son praised God and thanked Jesus for his kindness. Before starting away, the man asked him, "Who are you that God should answer your prayers?"

"If you adopted a son, could you not give him any inheritance you wanted to give him? What if your son asked for food? Would you give him a stone? I ask my Father for His glory, and He provides."

"Do you mean to say you are the Lord's adopted Son? Are you the anointed of David?"

Jesus answered, "Yes, I am he."

"How long we have waited for you!" he said, embracing him. "I shall go and tell of you. I shall tell everyone the Anointed One has come!" The man left with his son to speak to all he knew.

Feeling nothing else needed to be spoken, the prophet grinned, handed Jesus another scroll filled with parables to memorize, and walked away alone.

A woman came to draw water from the well, and Jesus said, "Will you give me a drink?"

"I am a Samaritan, and you are a Jew. How can you ask me for a drink?" She filled her bucket and gave him all he wanted.

"If you would ask me, I would give you living water that would well up to eternal life. Do you believe what I have said?"

"Such talk may be difficult for me to accept, though I have been told a Christ will someday come who will give eternal life."

"I am a Christ."

"That may also be difficult for me to accept."

"Yes, I know, but if it will help you, it is sometimes difficult for me to accept." He walked away, reading the scroll.

One afternoon, Jesus found himself walking through Nazareth. He stopped before an ornament maker's shop where shoppers were busy with discussion. They quieted when he stood among them, seemingly out of place.

"The first will be last, and the last will be first. To them who come to me, I shall forgive their sins. To those who do not, I shall forgive nothing."

They became offended at him and angered. "What do you mean you will forgive our sins? Only God can forgive sins."

Jesus answered, "I am to be a king, and a king's kingdom is his home. Before you allow anyone into your home, must you not forgive their wrongful ways? So too, must I forgive the wrongful ways of those seeking to live in my kingdom. Therefore, if you believe in me, I shall forgive your sins."

They became enraged and moved toward him, picking up stones to throw. "We know who you are!" they shouted. "You are the carpenter who is always making trouble. We know how sinfully you have lived your life. Be gone from us, you blaspheming hypocrite!" They began hurling stones at him, but Jesus ran away.

Later in Nazareth, Jesus went into a synagogue on Sabbath day. He stood and interrupted the proceedings to read from the scroll of Isaiah. "'The spirit of the Lord God is upon me because the Lord has anointed me to bring good news to the afflicted; He has sent me to bind up the brokenhearted, to proclaim liberty to captives and freedom to prisoners; to proclaim the favorable year of the Lord.'"

Then he sat down and said to them, "Today this Scripture has begun to be fulfilled in your hearing."

The worshipers asked one another, "Is this not Mary's son?" They became enraged at him for speaking in such a manner and caused him to leave Nazareth.

CHAPTER 7

At the start of a new week, many caravans had arrived in Jerusalem to trade. Their basket trunks were bursting with frankincense, myrrh, jewelry, and silks. They quickly spread their pottery and handicrafts on blankets for the eagerly awaited bargaining ritual. Caravans had been joined by people from distant places to stay safe during dangerous journeys through badlands with thieves and hostile tribes. Many had heard of a Jerusalem man and his healing powers since talk of him had spread from caravan to caravan. They came by mule and camel, dragging litters filled with the sick and lame. It was a hope for loved ones, however faint, for Jews and Gentiles alike.

Jesus came to them, healing their sick and demon-possessed, cleansing them of infirmity, and telling them about his kingdom. He was considered both magical and divinely blessed by God, for never was there such a person to perform such miraculous works and speak so boldly. Throngs of believers surrounded him so greatly he was no longer visible. Because so many people yearned to touch and hold him, it took hours for him to walk the length of one block. Some cried out to him by name; some cried out "Messiah" as they competed for his attention. His strength and confidence grew, nourished by their belief, which opened him to allow God's healing power to work among them.

On Sabbath day, many excited people went to the temple for worship after seeing miraculous healings. There was fervor in the crowd, stimulated by an expectancy of ending their Roman oppression. They sat as patiently as possible throughout the ceremony, anxiously waiting for the priests to speak of the beginning of restoration. When nothing was said, they grew restless and cried out, "Tell us of the Lord's kingdom; has not Shiloh come?"

At this, the priests became alarmed and answered them, "Why do you speak so? The Messiah has not yet come."

A woman stood before the assembly and called to them, "The Messiah has come! He has come! See how I stand without a crutch," she said, waving her arms, for she had been a cripple.

An old man stood as well to give testimony. "See how the leprosy has been taken away from me," he said, showing his arms. "The man called Jesus has healed me and many others where I live."

"How can this be when everything continues as before?" the priests questioned.

"I do not know," the old man answered. "All I can say is I had leprosy, yet now I am made clean."

"Jesus is healing the sick and insane," they cried out. "Jesus should be the high priest! Let Jesus be the high priest! See how God is with him."

The priests went to huddle together for discussion as they grew alarmed when the crowd became angry. The people had come with tremendous hope and expectancy of having their land rid of foreign enemies and receiving the promises made to their ancestors. They quieted as the high priest stepped from his counsel.

"The man called Jesus has deceived you. He is a practitioner of sorcery, and no good achievement can come from him. There have been such men, yet you immediately seek to make him king. How easy it is for you to be fooled. I am the high priest in this temple. It is I who should know the Messiah when I see him. Now go and do not let me hear any more of such talk."

The people left very dissatisfied. They congregated outside the temple, muttering in discontent, for what they had heard was not what they wanted to hear. The high priest watched from a distance, cautious enough to peer out of a half-opened door, not wanting to be seen.

When John heard what Jesus was doing, he sent his disciples to ask, "Are you the one who was to come, or should we expect someone else?"

Jesus replied, "Go back and tell John what you see. The lame walk, the blind see, and the poor have the gospel preached to them. Blessed are those who wait for the Branch of Jessie, for he shall reveal greater signs and wonders."

One day, Jesus was returning home from work he found at a construction site. He began to pass some men resting by their mules and became the center of their attention as all three turned to notice. His passing started laughter among them when one called out. "Ragged man!" he said, between his laughter. "Are you not the king of the Jews? Should we bow to you, Your Majesty?" They fell on their backs in raucous mockery. Jesus turned to notice while he continued to walk away. "Ragged man!" the taunter called again. "Tell us of your kingdom." They laughed heartily, holding their sides while gasping for breath. It was enough for Jesus to become enraged, as the day had been long and the sun very hot. He turned around and went toward them, clenching his fists by his side.

"I don't care what you believe!" He shouted with a severity they found alarming enough to stop their teasing. "I'm sick and tired of you all! I'm sick and tired of being spat on and mocked! I wouldn't mind getting rid of the entire lot of you!"

He stood over them; his feet dug firmly into the ground; his fists were still locked in anger. An expression of alarm came over their faces; they stopped smiling.

"You people make me disgusted! I'm beginning to regret starting this whole affair!" He turned and stormed away, continuing in his direction. They watched as he got farther away, saying nothing for fear he might return.

He crossed a large grassy plateau that helped to make the sky appear stretched at the ends. He kicked at the grass as he walked, mumbling and growling to himself. Having lost his temper, he was disappointed with himself, as that was something he was trying to control.

The walk did him no good as his legs grew tired, and his frustration heightened. He came upon a tree and, seeking its fruit's moisture, picked a portion to eat. He hungrily bit off its meat and, tasting its sourness, violently spit out the fruit. Again he vented his anger.

"Curse you, tree!" He threw the fruit at its trunk and started away when he realized he was still unsatisfied. He looked over his shoulder to shout again as if the tree could hear him. "I want you to dry up and die!"

By the time he returned home, the sun had all but disappeared. Jesus filled himself with bread and wine; seeking rest, he reclined to be alone with his thoughts. Jesus was always alone with his thoughts. He was never again to travel down that road, nor would he ever see the men who had scoffed at him. His window framed a picturesque setting sun that reddened the sky and released the early stars. He gazed without blinking at its wonderment and was entrenched in fear, pondering the newly acquired responsibility of it all and the fearful realization of what was soon to come.

One day thereafter, Jesus and the prophet were in a market area filled with shoppers and merchants eager to compete. The sun made it favorable to walk in only shaded areas, which had a way of taking them where they never expected to go. They browsed aimlessly from merchant to merchant, choosing to examine their wares as an excuse to stay under their awnings. There was plenty of casual talk to help fill an idle afternoon.

"What have you heard from your family lately? Word must have reached them by now of what you are doing," the prophet said.

"I have not heard from them since I left home. I have become too much of an embarrassment for them. They are very well-known, and many people have begun to talk."

"I'm sure you expected people would talk about you."

"Yes, I was prepared for the worst."

"It is good that they talk; at least you are getting known."

"I'm getting known, so much so that my family cast me out."

"What about your mother? Has she anything to say?"

"Even my mother does not understand; all my relatives believe I have lost my wits. I have become their shame. We seem to fight every evening. I mean, with my brothers and sisters. That is why I left. It all became unbearable." The crowd took his attention. "Look there, across the way. I know that man; he used to come with us. Let's turn here. I'd rather not see him," Jesus said, turning away.

"What do you say when you meet with your old friends?"

"I try to avoid them. It is very uncomfortable to speak with them now. They laugh when they see me coming. A few asked me to join them."

"You must not fall back into the temptation of your old life."

"No, of course not. I have no intentions of joining them again."

"Look at the temple. There is a lot of activity today."

"I see some priests are still doing their chores. It's unusual to find them here at this hour," Jesus said.

"This gives me an idea. Why don't you go on the temple mount and cause a ruckus in front of the priests? Turn over the merchants' carts and tables and throw the money changers out of the courtyard since they do not belong there anyway. That would really stir them into anger. Go on, make a big scene."

"What for? They might call the soldiers."

"Might nothing. They certainly will. Only we will be long gone by the time they arrive."

"What's the sense of such behavior?"

"We have to give them something to remember you by, a little antagonism to season the pot. That should get them good and mad at you."

"If I must be crucified to pay for my sins and wrongful doings, why don't I just walk up to the Romans and have them place me on a cross and be done with it? Why bother to involve anyone else?"

"Because even Romans don't go around killing people without a reason. There has to be someone to present a charge."

"How about if I were to walk in and confess to something? Wouldn't this whole ministry be over?"

"No, it wouldn't. They would not believe you, for no Jew would confess anything to a Roman. If they did, other people might believe it was true. Then how would they ever realize prophecy has come to pass that God has chastised you by 'the rod of men and the strokes of the sons of men'? They would say you suffered because of Roman law and not God's chastising. You must find your way to the cross innocently. Then the world would know they are much closer to receiving their Messiah."

"Why don't you just nail me to a tree if death is the punishment I am to have and be done with all this?" Jesus said, in frustration.

"Because public shame is part of the punishment, which I'm sure will remove the pride out of you forevermore. Further, doing it in this manner for an innocent man who has committed no wrong against the state, still condemned to die, will be seen as punishment from the hand of God."

"God certainly moves in mysterious ways. In all my miserable life, I never would have dreamed I would be doing this. The forces directing a man to change his path are certainly strange. Very well, if it must be, then it must be."

"Come, let us go on the mount while there is a crowd."

They made their way to the temple mount, where business was being conducted as usual. Dove sellers, jewelers, potters, and weavers frantically sought the attention of temple-goers. Jesus stood among them to assess their dealings. Then, suddenly approaching the traders' carts, he quickly turned them over.

"My Father's house is a house of prayer, yet you have turned it into a den of thieves!" he said, releasing the captive birds.

"I have seen your evil doings; I know of your wickedness!"

He grabbed a rope and, after fashioning it into a whip, began lashing at the people. "Get out of my house! Get out!"

A merchant who had watched his pottery being broken approached Jesus as if to attack him. Jesus smashed his fist into the man and knocked him to the ground, then thrashed the merchant violently about his body with the whip.

"Do you think I do not know what you do in this place?"

The man squirmed on the ground, trying to avoid any further beating. Then Jesus grabbed him by his clothing and threw him on a pile of vegetables.

"Stop that! You stop that!" said another merchant, trying to protect his valuables.

Jesus backhanded him across the face, knocking him to the ground. "Do you think you are too old to be beaten?" Jesus said, and began whipping him.

"Call the soldiers! Call the soldiers! He is a crazy man!" they said. Many in the crowd had moved away, not wanting to get involved. The younger boys, who worked for the merchants, quickly scurried for the authorities.

The prophet came forward, stumbling over the wreckage.

"Come on, let's go!"

They both ran into the street and disappeared into a winding maze of alleyways and buildings.

At this time, they celebrated King Herod's birthday. All the appointed authorities of the land had been invited to his birthday dinner and visiting dignitaries from Rome. The daughter of Herodias danced for the occasion, pleasing the palace guests and Herod himself.

So grateful did Herod become that he swore to give her anything she dared to ask to have. Being encouraged by her mother, she answered him, "Give me the head of John the Baptist on a platter." Because of the oath he had sworn before his guests, he was obliged to consent to her request, even though it grieved him, for he had come to respect John. His soldiers were sent to execute the one who had baptized Jesus, and his head was brought and laid at the feet of Herodias.

When John's disciples heard of his death, they came to claim his remains and buried him with his fathers. Later, they found Jesus and told him of the death. When he heard such news, he became distraught, as John was his first committed and the first to die for him. Jesus carried the grief of John's death with him as he traveled to an isolated place to be alone.

When the period of mourning was over, he returned to the prophet's home, where they talked about his ministry. The hours passed into evening; their time was given to prayer and study. The prophet then completed the evening's tutoring by putting away his writings. "Now is the right time to acquire people to help you teach of your kingdom; it will also fare well to have close followers. What happened to those fishermen we met at the shore?"

"I have not seen them for a long time," Jesus said. "I know they must be busy with their own lives and supporting their families. They became amazed for a time when they saw the miraculous healings, but none of them asked to remain with me on a daily basis."

"People are especially moved for reasons of personal gain. If you made them feel they were working toward something for themselves, their attitudes toward you would change. Why don't you offer them positions of high station in your kingdom? I'm sure they will be satisfied with such a reward. As they have seen and believed in your healing power, they will have to believe in your promise of a kingdom. You will have acquired a staff of workers as any true king should have."

"Very well, I will go down to the shore tomorrow."

"Remind them you will need help governing sections of your domain."

"What if they do not follow? What then?"

"We'll just find someone else," the prophet said, seeing Jesus to the door.

Jesus left and began walking alone into the darkness, deep in thought over what he had learned and what lay before him.

Sunrise made the day seem like any other and awakened the birds to help the morning along. Boat owners ritually prepared their ropes and tackles, displaying confidence in their fishing ability by their casualness. The breeze could never come too early or be too full for the many small boats needing a shove to open waters. Jesus maneuvered his way around an array of objects prone to decorate piers. A cool breeze momentarily cleansed his nostrils of fish smells and rotting planks. The wharf creaked beneath him, making it impossible to sneak up on anyone.

Peter and his brother Andrew were working on their boat, making repairs. They heard his footsteps approaching over their hammering. They greeted one another as they were joined by James and John, sons of Zebedee. Jesus sat on some crates and waited for them to do the same. He leaned toward them to capture their attention.

"I have come with good news, my friends. Considering the kingdom I shall have and the vast responsibility of governing its domain, I seek help overseeing its many branches of state. This is why I have sought you out. I am prepared to give you appointments to rule with me in my realm. This I offer in return for your belief in me and your loyalty. Together we will govern forever under the precepts of the Lord God, in light of His everlasting glory and before the radiance of His presence."

They did not doubt what future glory he might receive, for their memory served them well regarding the feats of miraculous healings he had performed, and they knew God had been with him.

"We are fishermen," they said. "What do we know about ruling a kingdom?"

"If you follow me, I will make you fishers of men and will ask the Lord God to grant you the gift of wisdom. I will pray you are given the strength you need to serve me well."

They looked at one another, astounded by what they heard. It did not take long to accept such an offer, and they agreed to follow him. In faith, they left their boats to go with him into the city to preach, foregoing the day's fishing.

Appearing before the many and the few, Jesus spoke as someone with authority. He went, preaching the gospel of salvation and healing all sickness among the people, saying, "Repent, for the kingdom of Heaven is at hand."

Day by day, news spread of his mighty teachings and deeds. Multitudes of people from Galilee, Decapolis, Jerusalem, Judea, and beyond the Jordan greeted him and gathered to listen to his oracles.

There had come other men he had approached to become officers in his kingdom.

He taught them while he taught the crowds as the fervor of excitement spread across the land. Never did the sons of Israel feel so close to receiving the promises God had made to Abraham. There was a revival of faith as they cherished his words, waiting to hear how their nation would be restored and their enemies defeated.

"You are the salt of the earth, but if the salt has become tasteless, how will it be made salty again? It could only be discarded and trampled underfoot by men. You are the light of the world. A city set on a hill cannot be hidden. Nor do men light a candle and put it where it cannot be seen but place it high for all to see. Let your light shine before men in such a manner that they may see your good works and glorify your Father who is in Heaven. Do not think I have come to abolish the law or the prophets; I did not come to abolish but to fulfill. For I say to you, until Heaven and Earth pass away, not the smallest measure of the law shall pass away until all has been fulfilled. Whoever then disobeys the smallest part of these commandments and so teaches others shall be called least in the kingdom of Heaven, but whoever keeps and teaches them shall be called great in the kingdom of Heaven. I say to you, unless your righteousness exceeds the scribes and Pharisees, you shall not enter the kingdom of Heaven.

"You have heard it said by your fathers, 'You shall not commit murder' and 'Whoever is guilty of murder will be liable to the court.' As well, I say to you, anyone angry with their brother shall be guilty before the court. Whoever shouts 'Raca' to his brother shall be guilty before a higher court, and whoever shouts, 'You fool!' will be near the fires of Hell. Therefore, if you bring an offering to the altar and suddenly remember your brother has something against you, leave your offering there before the altar and make amends with your brother. Learn to understand your adversary quickly lest he deliver you to the judge and from him to the guard who will throw you into prison. Truly I say to you, freedom shall not be yours until you have paid your entire debt. Indeed, those who sit in darkness in the dungeon never expected to be there, yet their Savior shall release them into the light of life.

"You have heard it said, 'You shall not commit adultery,' but I say to you that anyone who looks at a woman with lust has committed adultery in his heart. If your eye offends you, pluck it out and cast it away, for it is better for one part of your body to perish than for your whole body to be thrown into Hell. Likewise, if your hand causes you to stumble, cast it from you, lest you cause your soul to be consumed.

"It has been said, 'Whoever sends his wife away, let him offer a certificate of divorce,' but I say to you, any man who divorces his wife, except for disobedience, causes her to commit adultery, and whoever marries a woman who was wrongly divorced commits adultery.

"As well, it was told by your fathers: 'You shall not make false vows, but shall fulfill your vows to the Lord.' I say to you, do not swear at all, not by Heaven, for it is the throne of God, nor by the earth, for it is His footstool, nor by Jerusalem, for it is the city of the great king. Let your 'yes' be 'yes' and your 'no' be 'no'; anything beyond this comes from the evil one.

"When giving alms, do not sound a trumpet before you, as the hypocrites do in the synagogues so that men may praise them. Truly, they have had their reward. When you give alms, do so in secret, and your Father, who sees in secret, will be proud.

"When you pray, do not imitate the hypocrites, for they like to stand out and be praised by men. Truly, they have received their reward. When seeking prayer, go into a room, close the door, and pray to your Father in secret so that your prayers will reach Him. While praying, do not use meaningless repetition as the Gentiles do, for they only suppose their repetition will have meaning. When you pray, say, 'Our Father who is in Heaven, hallowed be your name, your kingdom come, your will be done, on Earth as it is in Heaven. Give us this day our daily bread. Forgive us our sins as we forgive those who transgress against us; lead us away from temptation, and deliver us from evil, for yours is the kingdom and the power and the glory, forever, amen.' If you forgive men for their transgressions, your heavenly Father will forgive you. If you do not forgive men, your Father will not forgive your transgressions.

"When you fast, do not put on a sad front, as do the hypocrites, for they relish being seen by men. Truly, they have had their reward. When fasting, anoint your head and wash your face so that you will be unnoticed by men and seen by God.

"Do not strive to accumulate treasures on Earth where moths and rust destroy and thieves break in to steal. Seek first the kingdom of God, that is lasting, over those fleeting pleasures in this world you could acquire for yourself. Strive to build yourself treasures in Heaven so you may have them for life everlasting. Where your treasure is, there your heart be always. The eye is the light of the body; if your eye is fixed on heavenly goals, then your whole body will be filled with unquenchable light. You cannot serve two masters; either you will hate one or love the other. No one can serve both God and mammon.

"Do not be anxious for your life, as to food or drink, nor for your body or clothing. Isn't life more important than food and the body more than its clothing? See the birds of the air; they do not sow nor reap, yet their needs are met to suffice. Are you not worth more than they? Who can add an extra day to your life by being anxious? Sufficient for the day is the evil thereof. Seek first the kingdom of Heaven where all your needs shall be given to you.

"Do not judge, lest you be judged. In what manner you judge is what will be afforded you. Do not look at the speck in your brother's eye and ignore the log in your own eye.

"Ask and it shall be given you; seek and you shall find; knock and the door will open. Who among you will give your son a stone when he asks for food? If you then, being evil, know how to give gifts, how much more shall your heavenly Father give what is good to those who ask Him? Therefore, do unto others as you want others to do unto you.

"Know the gates of Heaven are narrow, and broad is the way leading to destruction, for surely many have already fallen there.

"Beware of false prophets who appear to you in sheep's clothing but inwardly are ravenous wolves. You shall know them by their fruits. Can harvesters pick grapes from thorns or figs from thistles? Only a good tree can bear good fruit; only a bad tree can bear bad fruit. Those trees bearing bad fruit are cut down and cast into the fire. A man is known by the fruit he bears. Not everyone who says to me, 'Lord, Lord,' will enter the kingdom of Heaven, but only those who do the will of my Father who is in Heaven. Many will say to me that day, 'Lord, did we not prophesy in your name and in your name cast out demons and perform miracles?' I will say to them, 'Be gone from me, for I never knew you.'

"Therefore, they who hear my words and live by them may be compared to a wise man who has built his house on rock. When the rains come, and the winds blow, it shall not fall, for it is based on the cornerstone of God. Everyone who hears my words and does not live by them will be like a foolish man who has built his house on sand. When the rain and wind come, it shall collapse the house along with everything in it."

While in the city, he was eating dinner with his followers in a tax collector's home. When the Pharisees and other teachers of the law saw this, they said to his followers, "How can this Jesus, who sits with and is one of these thieves, drunkards, and gamblers, claim to be a Messiah all of a sudden?" The followers had no answer. Later, they asked Jesus what they should have said. He told them, "I have not come to call the righteous but sinners."

In the meal hour of the next day, Jesus and his followers were eating in an inn and talking among themselves. The inn was a gathering place for caravan travelers, residents, and Roman soldiers. The room was alive with conversation and a blend of languages only expected in a city that was a center for trade. Soldiers entered and sat at a table across from Jesus and his friends. The soldiers, recognizing them as Jews, surrounded their table as they came to make sport of them. The largest soldier was the first to speak the expected insults.

"What foul odor do I smell?" He sniffed at the table. "Why don't you Jews go outside and eat with the rest of the swine?"

Jesus was sitting directly before him and, without hesitation, splashed his goblet of wine into the soldier's face, then jumped to his feet and began smashing him with his fists. His friends then rose and lunged at the Romans. When Jesus was finished with the first soldier, he jumped into the melee that had started and threw a soldier against a wall as the inn's patrons scurried out of the way. No one dared interfere with their fighting. After the soldiers were defeated, Jesus and his followers ran from the inn, leaving the soldiers among the rubble.

CHAPTER 8

When Jesus entered Capernaum, a centurion came to him, asking for help. "Lord, my servant lies at home paralyzed and in pain."

Jesus said, "I will go with you and heal him."

The centurion refused, saying, "Lord, I am not worthy of you to come beneath my roof. Just say the word, and my servant will be healed. I am a man of authority, having soldiers beneath me. When I say 'go,' they go; if I say 'come,' they come. Should I say to my slave, 'do this,' he does it."

After hearing this, Jesus became impressed and said, "Truly, I say to you, I have not found such faith in all of Israel. There will come a time when those of faith will gather from the east and west to recline at the table with Abraham, Isaac, and Jacob in the kingdom of Heaven, but those of little faith will be cast into the pit of darkness where there is weeping and gnashing of teeth."

Turning to the centurion, he said, "Go your way; I shall ask my Father that as you believe, so may it be done." When the centurion returned home, he found his servant restored and waiting for him at the door.

Jesus entered Peter's home and saw Peter's mother-in-law lying sick with a fever in bed. He touched her hand, and the fever left immediately, permitting her to rise. She waited on him for the rest of his stay. When people nearby heard where he was, they brought the demon-possessed and sick, and he cast out the spirits with a word. He healed all who were ill so that it might come to pass what the prophet Isaiah said of him, "He took away our infirmities and healed us of our diseases."

Arriving at Gadarenes, two men who were demon-possessed met him as they came out of their caves. Normally, their violence prohibited anyone from passing on that road. They cried out to him, "What do you want with us, Son of God? Have you come here to torture us before the appointed time?" Noticing a herd of pigs feeding a short distance away, they begged, "If you wish to send us away, send us into the herd of pigs."

He answered them, "Go forth then into the pigs." They came out and entered the pigs, and the entire herd ran down a steep bank into a lake and drowned. When those tending the flock saw this, they ran to their village to tell everyone of the pigs and the demon-possessed men. When Jesus walked by them, they pleaded with him to leave quickly, fearing the evil legions would make it worse for them if they allowed him to stay.

Returning to his city, he saw a group of men bringing him a paralytic who was lying on a bed. Seeing their faith, he addressed the paralytic, "Your sins are forgiven."

Some scribes said to themselves, "This man blasphemes."

Recognizing the scorn on their faces, Jesus said, "Why do you think evil in your hearts? Amen, which is easier to say, 'Your sins are forgiven,' or 'Rise and be whole'? I will grant mercy so you may know the Son of Man has authority over all wonders." He turned to the paralytic. "Be healed; take up your bed and go home." The paralytic stood before everyone and caused many people to believe the gospel.

When John's disciples found Jesus in the city, they asked, "Why do we and the Pharisees fast, but your disciples do not fast?"

Jesus said to them, "How can friends of the bridegroom mourn when the bridegroom is with them? There shall come a day when the bridegroom will be taken away; then they shall have cause to fast. You would not put a new patch on an old garment, for the patch will pull away, causing a worse tear. Nor would you put a lot of wine into old wineskins, for they will burst. They wait for me to be made anew."

While he was speaking, an official bowed to him, saying, "My daughter has just died. Come and touch her so that she may be restored."

They went with him to restore the child, and as they departed, a woman who gave forth blood for twelve years approached him from behind and touched his cloak. She said, "If I only touch his cloak, I will be healed." Feeling her hand, Jesus turned and spoke, "Daughter, your belief has made you well." The woman knew she was healed the moment she heard his words.

They arrived at the official's home, which was in mourning. Jesus entered, saying, "Send the mourners away, for the girl is not dead; she is asleep." They scoffed at him for saying that but watched as he took her hand and helped her to her feet.

Continuing through the cities and towns, he taught in the synagogues, wherever welcomed, proclaiming the gospel of salvation and healing every kind of disease and those who were demon-possessed. Seeing the multitudes, he was moved with compassion, for they were weary and forlorn like sheep without a shepherd. He went to his disciples, saying, "The harvest is plentiful, but the workers are few. Pray with me to ask the Lord God for more shepherds to bring in His harvest."

The prophet saw the throngs of people pushing against one another to get to the front and said to Jesus, "I never anticipated you would have acquired such a following so quickly. This is truly the work of God."

His disciples approached him to explain that many had asked if he were John the Baptist returned to life or the prophet spoken of by Moses. Jesus asked Peter, "Who do you say I am?"

Peter answered, "You are a Christ, adopted Son of the living God."

Jesus said, "Blessed are you, Peter, for believing. On such faith, I will build my church."

Then he told his twelve disciples, "In my name, you will pray to God that He might cast out evil spirits and heal disease and sickness. I send you out into the world to preach of me. Do not go where the Gentiles live nor where the Samaritans are. Rather, find the lost sheep of the house of Israel. Pray for their sick, diseased, and unclean. As you receive freely, you are to give freely. Take no purse, gold, or silver with you. Do not pack your bag with coats, sandals, or blankets, for if you are true, all will be provided for you.

When you enter a town, seek only those worthy of you and abide with them. Greet each home you enter. Greet all with my peace and understanding, but should they prove themselves unworthy, reclaim your greeting and depart. Whoever does not welcome you does not welcome me, for I have sent you. Have nothing more to do with them, even to the point of shaking off their dust from your feet.

"I am sending you out as sheep before wolves. Therefore, be shrewd as serpents and innocent as doves. Be cautious of all men; if they had their way, they would deliver you to the authorities to be scourged and shamed. You will be directed before governors and kings for my name as a testimony to them and the Gentiles. When you find yourself before them, do not fret over what you will say, for the spirit of your Father will give you the strength you need to speak.

"Brother will go as far as betraying his brother to death and a father against his child; children will rebel against their parents if it would help them destroy you. All men will hate you because of me, but all who stand firm to the end will be saved.

"A disciple is not above his teacher, and a slave is not above his master. If the head of the household has been called 'Beelzebub,' how much more will be the members of the household? Therefore, do not fear them. There is nothing concealed that will not be revealed and hidden that will not be known. What you hear in darkness, speak in the light; what you hear whispered in your ear, shout from the rooftops. Do not fear those who kill the body but cannot kill the soul. Rather, fear Him, who can destroy both the soul and body. Are you not permitted to buy two sparrows for a farthing? Yet not one of them can fall to the ground apart from the will of your Father. God is with you always and has numbered the very hairs on your head. Therefore, do not fear; are you not of more value than sparrows?

"Be there anyone who confesses me before men, I will confess them before my Father who is in Heaven. Whoever shall deny me before men, I will also deny them before my Father who is in Heaven. Do not think I have come to bring peace to the earth. I do not come to bring peace but a sword. I have come to place father against son and mother against daughter. A man's enemies will be the members of his household. They who love their disbelieving father or mother more than me are not worthy of me; they who love their disbelieving son or daughter more than me are not worthy of me as well. Nor is anyone worthy of me if they refuse to take up their cross. They who find their life shall lose it, yet they who lose their life for my sake shall find it. Anyone who receives you receives me, and they who receive me receive Him who sent me. They who receive a prophet in the name of a prophet will receive a prophet's reward; they who receive a righteous person in the name of a righteous person will receive a righteous person's reward. Those who give so much as a cup of water to a child in the name of a disciple shall not lose their reward."

A man ran up to him, having seen his miracles, and knelt before him, asking, "Good teacher, what shall I do to inherit eternal life?"

Hearing such words, Jesus turned and snapped at him, "Don't call me good!" For he had been ashamed of his life. "When have I ever said I was good? Only God in Heaven is good. You know the commandments: 'Do not murder, do not commit adultery, do not steal, do not bear false witness, do not defraud, and honor your father and mother.'"

He answered, "Rabbi, I have kept these laws all my life."

"One chore you lack," Jesus said, "go and sell your possessions and follow me."

The man could not hold up his face any longer and went away sad, for he was a man of wealth. Jesus looked around, saying to the people, "Remember well, it is easier for a camel to go through the eye of a needle than for a lover of money to enter the kingdom of God."

After Jesus finished instructing his twelve disciples, he taught and preached in the towns of Galilee. There he condemned the cities where many of his miracles were done.

"Woe to you, Chorazin! Woe to you, Bethsaida! If the mighty works done in your sight had been done in Tyre and Sidon, they would have repented long ago. I tell you, it will be more tolerable for Tyre and Sidon on the day of judgment than for you. Nor will

God look away from the sins of Capernaum. If the miracles were given before Sodom's eyes that were given to your eyes, it would be thriving today; you shall be cast into a burning fire."

Coming to a group of children, he said, "I thank you, my Father, Creator of Heaven and Earth; you have concealed these wonders from the wise and learned, yet revealed them to these children. All of creation will soon be presented unto me by my Father. No one comes to the Son unless the Father so allows; you have not asked for belief in me, yet ask in my name, and you will receive. Henceforth, any belief you ask for in my name, you will receive.

"Come to me all you who are weary, for I will give rest to your soul and mind. Receive the yoke on you God has placed on me and learn of me. You, too, shall be made gentle and humble of heart."

A man of the Pharisees named Nicodemus came to Jesus in secret, saying, "Rabbi, I know you are a teacher from God, for no man can do these miracles if he were outside of God."

Jesus favored him, saying, "Verily, verily, unless you are born again, you cannot see the kingdom of God."

"How can a man be born when he is old? He cannot enter a second time into a womb, can he?"

"Unless one is born of water and spirit," Jesus said, "they cannot enter the kingdom of God. That which is born of the flesh is flesh; that which is born of the spirit is spirit. Do not be surprised I have said, 'You must be born again.' The wind blows where it wishes. You hear it passing, yet do not know where it comes from or where it is going, so it is with those born of the spirit."

Nicodemus questioned, "How can such teachings be?"

"You are a teacher of Jews, and you say you do not understand? Truly, I speak of splendors given by my Father and have always spoken outright, yet you have not received my testimony. As I have told you earthly concerns and you refuse to believe, how do you expect to understand heavenly concerns? As Moses lifted the serpent in the wilderness, even so, must the Son of Man be lifted. For God so loved the world, He has sent His Son, that whoever receives him shall not perish but have eternal life. God has not sent His Son into the world to condemn the world, but that the world will be saved through him. They who receive me are not condemned, yet they who do not receive have been judged already, for they do not believe in the king of the heavenly realm. Such is their damnation that the light has come into the world, and they love darkness over light because their deeds are evil. Everyone who lives in evil hates the light and dares not come near lest their deeds be exposed. They who practice the truth come closer to the light so that their deeds may be manifested as having been rooted in God."

One day thereafter, the prophet found Jesus sleeping in an alleyway, as Jesus no longer had a place to stay and was not one to ask for charity. The prophet awoke Jesus to ask what he was doing there, and he answered, "The birds have their nests, the foxes, their dens, but the Son of Man has nowhere to lay his head."

"Why did you not tell me you had nowhere to live?" the prophet said, and took Jesus home with him.

CHAPTER 9

There came a Sabbath when Jesus and his disciples traveled through a grain field and, being hungry, picked the grain and ate. When the Pharisees saw them, they complained to Jesus, saying, "Why do you allow your disciples to break the law on Sabbath?"

"Do you not remember what David did when he became hungry? He entered the house of God and ate consecrated bread, being saved for the priests. Do you not know that the priests in the temple break the Sabbath and are innocent? So look around you; do you not see something greater than the temple before you? Had you any understanding of what I have said, 'I desire compassion and not sacrifice,' you would not have condemned the innocent. Know also that the Son of Man shall be made Lord of the Sabbath."

Departing from there, he went into their synagogue. There, he saw a man with a withered hand. The Pharisees began questioning him, saying, "Is it lawful to heal a man on Sabbath?" They said this hoping to accuse him.

"Who among you is there who has a sheep fallen into a pit on a Sabbath and does not take it out? How much greater is a man over a sheep? Thus, it is lawful to do good on a Sabbath." Then he said to the man, "Stretch out your hand." When the man complied, he saw his hand restored. Having been corrected in front of everyone, the Pharisees departed and planned with one another how to discredit Jesus.

Then a demon-possessed man who was also blind and mute was brought to him to be healed. When the crowd saw this happen, they said, "Could this be the true son of David who was to come?" When the Pharisees saw their opportunity, they interrupted, claiming, "This man casts out demons by the power of Beelzebub, the prince of devils."

Jesus came forth to defend himself. "Any kingdom divided against its own is laid to ruin, for a house divided against itself cannot stand. If the devil is of mind to divide himself, how will it be possible for his legions to rule? Whereas I cast out demons by the will of God, it serves as a sign to you that the kingdom of God is near to come. If you had eyes, you would see. Whereas you do not, I perceive the kingdom of Heaven is not for you. Go your way to enjoy what is left of your life, for it is all the life you will receive."

Some scribes and Pharisees became frightened of him and asked, "Show us a greater sign."

Jesus answered, "The more evil in a generation, the greater a sign they crave. I say no sign will be given but that of Jonah, the prophet. Just as Jonah dreamed he was three days in the belly of a fish, so shall the Son of Man be three days in the heart of the earth, only actually so. Then I shall rise from the dead after the third day for the glory of God. The people of Nineveh will stand up at the judgment with this generation and condemn it, for they eagerly repented before Jonah's preaching, and now one greater than Jonah is here, even I.

"When an evil spirit comes out of a person, it goes out seeking rest, but does not find it, so it says, 'I will return to the house I left.' When it returns, it sees the house finely decorated and clean. Then it goes and takes seven other spirits eviler than itself, and they all inhabit there. Finally, the person is worse off than before. That is how it will be for this generation."

While he was addressing them, his brothers arrived and attempted to get close to see him. As they could not get ahead of the many who congregated around Jesus, they sent a messenger who approached, saying, "Your brothers are outside, wanting to see you. They are here to take you away by force if they must because they believe you insane."

Jesus answered, pointing to his disciples, "Here are my brothers. Whoever does the will of my Father in Heaven shall be my brother and my sister."

Still needing an answer, the messenger said, "That may be well and good, but what do I tell your brothers? They claim you are responsible for the death of your cousin John and say they want no more grief over your foolish babbling."

"Tell them nothing," Jesus said, turning aside. "They will get tired as usual and go away."

That evening he went to the sea. Crowds of people followed to entreat him to heal their infirmities and to hear more of his teaching. Getting into a boat, he moved out before them as they sat on the beach. He addressed them in parables, saying, "Behold, a sower went forth to sow; some of his seeds fell beside the road, and the birds came and ate them. Other seeds fell on the rocks to be scorched by the sun and, having no roots, were blown away. Other seeds fell among thorns. When the weeds grew, they choked them out. Some seeds fell on good soil to produce fruit in abundance."

His disciples asked, "Why do you speak in parables?"

"To you, permission has been granted to understand the mysteries of Heaven, but to them, permission has not been granted. Whoever has, to them more will be given; yet to those who do not have, even what little they have will be taken away. If knowledge were for them to have, knowledge would be revealed; if they are not to know, knowledge shall not be revealed. This is why I speak in parables: while seeing, they do not see, while listening, they do not hear. Blessed are you for having eyes and ears to understand. Even the prophets of old and all the many righteous who craved to understand were not able to have what you have received this day."

They were still puzzled by the way he spoke to them, so he said, "Hear the parable of the sower. When anyone hears the words regarding Heaven and does not understand, the evil ones come to steal away that which was planted in their heart. This is the one whose seed had fallen beside the road. Those of Earth who have no firm root in themselves are like the seeds that fall on the rocks; when the winds come, they are blown away easily. The ones who receive the seeds that fell among thorns are they who hear the word, yet the cares of life and zest for vain glory choke them to unfruitfulness. The ones who had seeds fall on good soil hear the word and understand it and, consequently, bring forth abundant fruit."

He presented another parable, "The kingdom of Heaven is like a mustard seed which someone took and planted. Though it is smaller than any other seed, if properly nourished, it will grow into a full-sized tree."

He went on talking to his disciples and the crowds, speaking in parables as instructed, teaching all who cared to listen. After he left, several people lingered to discuss his teachings. Some of them ran to catch up to the prophet as they noticed he traveled with Jesus.

"Tell us," they asked, "why does your rabbi say to forgive our brother seven times seven and yet say God Himself will not forgive us if we do not abide in His Son? Why should the Lord God ever stop caring for the sons of Israel? This Jesus is saying words he should not say."

The prophet sat with them, for he saw they were sincere in asking. "Know Jesus has never lied to you. He has always spoken the truth concerning who he is, what he is, and what will happen. He is like you and me in every way and has shared his portions of grief with no one. The devil and his minions have seen to it there was never anyone around to support him. Know also that man has in his heart both evil and good. Indeed, man should forgive his brother seven times seven. As man can forgive, so will God forgive a thousandfold more. While man dwells on Earth, he shall have the Lord's forgiveness. If a man breathes his last breath while unprepared, he will discover in the next world he is as he was on Earth, stained and unforgiven. A butterfly cannot arrange its colors while in the cocoon. Once it leaves its cocoon, it cannot return. Man is like a butterfly; when he dies, he cannot return to Earth for a second chance. Yet man can change himself while on Earth, whereas the butterfly cannot. I ask you: Would you let me into your home if I arrived stained with filth?"

"No, of course not."

"Amen, you have answered your question."

They departed from him feeling satisfied and returned to their homes to tell others what they had learned.

When Jesus was preaching and healing at the Sea of Tiberius, his disciples said, "Send the crowds away, so they can go and buy themselves some food, for there is no food for them in this wilderness."

Jesus said, "What food do you have?"

"We have about five loaves of bread and two fish."

Jesus said, "Bring what you have to me and have the people rest on the ground."

He took the loaves and fish and blessed them. Then he broke the bread and gave the bread and fish to his disciples. They served those sitting on the ground, who numbered about five thousand men, besides women and children. The food not eaten was piled in baskets.

CHAPTER 10

Then came a day when Jesus found the prophet sitting alone beneath a tree and approached him.

"Let me ask you something, for I have been thinking," Jesus said. "If the prophets foresaw I would fall into and be numbered with the transgressors, why was there not someone around to guide me differently? Indeed, it is God's fault I fell into sin, for He had not given me enough strength."

"Tell me, how did you live your life?"

"I lived the way I wanted to live."

"Then it was your choice to follow the ways of man."

"I still feel God could have given me more support."

"Who is more qualified to know what a sufficient amount is more than God?"

Feeling disheartened, Jesus said, "What if I were to change my mind? What if I were to let someone else be the Messiah? Remember, I never asked for this ministry, and I never asked God to adopt me. It is hard enough for me to find work to support myself; now I have this ministry, that is nothing but burden. Most of the people I speak to think I'm a lunatic."

"Amen. The world will continue as it has, and there will be no Messiah. Nor would there ever be a kingdom of God on Earth; for if you do not come and go, your brother cannot come to restore your people and homeland, and the sick and lame, the hungry and lost, will have to continue fending for themselves."

"Oh, I see. I am made to feel responsible for them. Was it I who placed the world in such a state?"

The prophet said, "No, of course not. However, while it was not you who despoiled the earth, you will make it possible for it to be regained. Know that God is no respecter of persons, not even with His adopted Son." He started to leave when he reminded himself, "I know that as much as anyone. As I once said, there are other ways I would rather have spent my life than in the anguish it took to get me doing this." He handed Jesus another scroll to memorize and began walking away.

Jesus shouted after him, "I'm still not too happy about my life adding up to a grand sacrifice."

"You have said it right. It is a grand sacrifice indeed. The world will cherish what you have done," the prophet answered, and walked away.

When Jesus and his disciples came to the Sea of Galilee shore, he sat on some rocks where people approached to receive healing. There was much praise and glorifying of God that day when they saw the crippled restored, the blind seeing, and the dying made whole.

Jesus summoned his disciples, saying, "I am filled with compassion for the multitudes, for they have followed me many days and have nothing to eat."

His disciples said, "Where could we buy enough food to feed the many in this wilderness? They will faint from hunger if they are not sent away."

Jesus asked, "How many loaves do you have?"

"Seven," they replied, "and a few small fish."

Jesus took the loaves and fish and, giving thanks, prayed for the will of God to be done. He broke the bread and gave the bread and fish to his disciples, who gave them to the crowd. All of them ate until they were full. They picked up the leftovers, which filled seven baskets. The multitude had numbered about four thousand men, besides women and children; all had left thoroughly content.

The disciples questioned Jesus as they walked with him, saying, "Who is greatest in the kingdom of Heaven?"

He called a child, placed him in their midst, and said, "Verily, verily, unless you are converted and become like children, you shall not enter the kingdom of Heaven. They who humble themselves as this child will be considered greatest in Heaven. Whoever receives such a child in my name receives me. Whoever encourages these little ones, who believes in me to stumble, will find it better to have a millstone hung around their neck and to be drowned in the depths of the sea.

"If a man has a hundred sheep and one of them goes astray, would he not then rejoice over finding it over the ninety-nine which did not go astray? I tell you, it is not the wish of your heavenly Father that one of these little ones should perish."

He then told them another parable. "The kingdom of Heaven is like a farmer who hired laborers for his vineyard. He sent them into his vineyard to harvest after agreeing to pay each a denarius. At the third hour, he saw others idle in the market square and said, 'Work in my vineyard, and I will pay you as I will the others.' So, they went and harvested. Again he went out about the sixth and ninth hours and offered the same. At the eleventh hour, he found still more idle men and sent them into his vineyard. When evening came, he called in his laborers to pay the last group first; each was given a denarius. To those who were the first to harvest, he also gave a denarius. They began complaining. 'Have we not worked longer and harder? Should we not get more?' He said to them, 'Did I not tell you your wage would be a denarius? If I give the same amount to these men, what is that to you? Is it not legal for me to do what I desire with my wealth?' Thus, the last will be first, and the first will be last.

"Hear what I have told you, for soon I will be with you no longer. Though you still have much to learn, I have chosen twelve of you to take my message to the Jews and the Gentiles, yet one of you has become a devil. There will be many such others to discredit my Father and me, though on the day of judgment, there will be weeping and remorse, for remember, you reap what you sow." They talked among themselves regarding which one he was referring to who had become a devil.

Jesus continued until he came before a man who was blind from birth. His disciples asked him, "For this man to have been born blind, who sinned—the man or his parents?"

He answered them, "He is blind not because of his sin, nor his parents' sin, but that the glory of God could be shown in him." Then he made some mud from spittle and covered the blind man's eyes with it, saying to him, "Go wash in the pool of Siloam." He washed as he was told and returned healed of his blindness.

They who previously knew him as a blind man said, "Isn't he the one who sat and begged for a living?" Becoming very curious, they asked him, "Why are you able to see?"

He told them, "The man called Jesus of Nazareth put mud on my eyes and told me to wash in Siloam, so I did, and now I see." They went out to look for Jesus, but he had already left.

As they passed the temple area, one of his disciples commented, "Look at what beautiful buildings these are."

"Do you marvel at them?" Jesus said, "I tell you, not one stone will remain on another."

They went and rested at the Mount of Olives overlooking the temple area. His followers asked, "Tell us when such destruction will happen."

He told them and the crowd, "Be careful you are not deceived. Many will come in my name, saying, 'I am the Christ,' and will deceive many. You will hear of wars and rumors of wars, but be not troubled, for all these events must come to pass. The end has still to come. Race will rise up against race and kingdom against kingdom. There will be famines, pestilence, and earthquakes in various places. Such will be the beginning of birth pains. Many will fall away from their beliefs to betray and hate one another while false prophets will appear and deceive many. The love of most will grow cold because of excessive evil, yet they who stand firm to the end will be saved. The gospel of the kingdom will be preached to all nations, and then the end will come when the Son of Joseph and his prophet come to smite the world with plagues. Justice will be dealt accordingly, for the spirit of the Lord shall rest on him to make him a mighty arm of the Almighty. He will come as I have to speak on behalf of the Creator of Earth, wind, and fire. Bread and butter will not be the spoil, but starvation and torment will be rewarded. Men and women will kill saints in the name of God and expect a reward. Even the unborn will fight their birth because of the grief that lies in wait for them. He will rule nations with a rod of iron and come to condemn the world; woe be to the one who steps before him, as it is written, 'Kiss the Son, lest you perish in his way when his anger is kindled just a little.' The seed of Jessie will cause a horn to sound, gathering the dispersed tribes from the four corners to the shelter of Zion. He will come in my name, and many will be added to the fold, yet many will not. Righteousness will be a belt about his loins. With the breath of his lips, will he slay the wicked, for when he is exposed from the shadow of the Lord's hand, his mouth will be made like a sharpened sword. His recompense will be before him as restitution for his sorrows; anyone who does not listen to him will be called to account by the Lord God Himself.

"People will flee to caves from dread of the Lord and the splendor of his majesty when he rises to shake the earth. Mankind will be dragged along the path of woe; madness will grip the most civilized. They will foam at the mouth like demon dogs and slither on their bellies to hiss at their own young. In those days, people of every kindred and tongue will say, 'Let us find a Jew to hide behind.' Those living in the land beneath a shadow of death will see a light dawning, for he will enlarge the nation and increase their joy; nations will be torn beneath a tidal wave of fire; their remnants will fight in vain to regain the land. He will be called to the Holy Mountain to receive the word of the Lord, and his law will go forth into the world from Zion. They shall worship as their fathers did, presenting grain and burnt offerings. He shall deliver his people from the yoke of bondage, like unto Moses, and make himself an ensign to the nations. He will give his life for the fallen and forgive your sins so that you may come into his rest with everlasting redemption. Their bodies will be healed, their minds mended, made whole to the glory of God among them; at the age of a hundred, people will still run beside the gazelle.

"The staff of Moses will be raised again. Floods will be exchanged for drought; drought will be exchanged for floods. There will be other Passovers as in Egypt when the Angel of Death was sent to strike firstborn sons. Mothers will grieve, and fathers will groan. They shall weep the same as Egyptians. He will not judge one by what he sees or hears, yet will judge by what his Father both sees and hears. Nor will you be called Israel, for he will give Israel a new name you will sing from the mountaintops.

"Forces of Gog and Magog will mass against him in battle to strike him from his throne. As well, the chastisement of the Lord will be upon him. They will look upon the one they pierced and mourn as they would for an only child. The sheep will be scattered, and refining will commence as one purges gold in a furnace. He will be held up as the last banner, and those who choose to come into the fold may do so; then the gate will be closed, and those remaining will perish in the fire.

"He will have become more despised than any other man so that when he dies, the world will give gifts to one another in celebration. Understand that on the fourth day, he will rise and be taken up. The world will be given to its own iniquity, and desolation will bring forth vast travail. Then he will return from the clouds, one like the Son of Man, and every eye will see him, even those who pierced him; and all the people of the earth will mourn for themselves at the sight of him, for he had trodden the winepress of the fury of the wrath of God and will be hailed, King of kings and Lord of lords. His feet shall walk the Mount of Olives, and he shall fight as before, even more so, causing his enemies to be slain by the thousands.

"Peer across the sea; seek him in a foreign land of Gentiles. Listen as he speaks; he chastises the unrighteous and presents the anger of the Lord. He bends the bow to humble nations before him and spits on their pleading. The earth trembles at his footsteps; their cities are piled in rubble, given up to rats and lice; his whip shall peel the flesh from the backs of Egyptians to suffer them to toil.

"You will not have to ask, 'Are you the one?' You will know him when you see him, for what mortal man rides on the wings of fire? His garments will be stained crimson from the blood of nations and soaked with the stench of death. The earth is bruised from its trampling and moans when it is walked upon; it hurries night to be rid of day and hurries day to be rid of night. Everything on

Earth will be placed beneath his feet. All who are found in default are made to pay, and grim is the sight of the Reaper. The day of the Lord will be ugly and cursed by both the good and bad. The world will plot against him with every waking breath but will have no avail, as it was written, 'Why do the nations rage and the people plot in vain? The kings of the earth take their stand, and the rulers gather together against the Lord and against His Anointed One.'

"There will be a voice commanding, 'In the wilderness, make the way straight, a highway for our God. Every valley is to be raised, every hill lowered, the rugged places made smooth, and all mankind together will see the glory of the Lord being revealed when God descends from the mountaintop.' Fire will be called down to smite blasphemers and awaken disbelievers. Do not let sleep be an excuse to take your eyes away or let eating allow you to turn away from him for a moment, for in his shadow will the Redeemer of Israel appear, causing the sky to brighten from the joy of Abraham, Isaac, and Jacob. Soon I shall leave, and you will not see me again until you say, 'Blessed is he that comes in the name of the Lord.'

"In those days, a kingdom will form that will cause the farmers' baskets to spew abundance. The moon will shine like the sun, and there shall not be darkness on the earth. Never has there been such a kingdom, not even in children's dreams; the ark of Noah will come out of the clouds. New creatures without hate or envy, suffering, or emptiness will be formed. They will frolic for a hundred years, exhausting themselves with work and play, sleeping with unlocked doors and windows. There will be a new Adam and a new Eve among you; never will they cry in remorse nor cast a shadow of disbelief, for the light of God will shine through them. Land will appear where there is no land, and the young will be told stories of how man made war and malice, made grief and hunger, and the young will laugh in disbelief.

"Man will be restored to the early days with Earth divided into provinces, each to their own kind. Nor will there be one hungry person on planet Earth, nor one homeless or naked person. Should a tear fall, it will be heard worldwide, for one person's grief will be every person's grief. Should one smile, it will be felt around the world, for one person's joy will be every person's joy. No one will have what another does not. Those who commit a crime will send shock waves to all continents. Gold will be litter in the streets, and people will sing about God among them.

"To be banished from the kingdom will be seen as worse than death. Those who belong shall receive a mark that cannot fade or be erased, and they shall ride happily on the fatted calf. Men shall not know war; their swords will be beaten into plowshares. Prisons of stone and iron cages will be torn to the ground; their captives will be set free. There will be no poor, and there will be no rich, yet all will have the wealth of their king. Trees will be felled in great numbers to make way for new dwellings. Harvest season will bring everyone into the fields so that all can stock their bins to overflowing. The earth will not be alone in the endless expanse; even the most blind will see the glory of the Lord in the heavens.

"Know I have told you beforehand, for this reason, I have come into the world for you to believe in me that you might be raised on the last day to be with your fathers.

"Therefore, when you see the abomination that causes desolation, spoken of by the prophet Daniel standing in the holy place, they in Judea should flee to the mountains. Allow no one on the roof of his home to go down to retrieve anything out of the house. Woe be to those filled with child. Pray your flight is not in winter or on a Sabbath. For there will be great tribulation that has not occurred since the beginning of the world up to now, nor ever will. Unless those days are shortened, no life would be saved, yet for the sake of the elect, those days will be shortened. Should anyone say to you, 'Behold, here is Christ,' or 'Look over there for him,' do not believe it. False christs and prophets will arise and show signs and wonders, even in the attempt to deceive the elect. Know I have told you beforehand. If it is told you, 'Christ is in the desert,' do not believe it, or 'Look, he is in a retreat,' do not go there. As lightning comes from the east and flashes to the west, so will the coming of the Son of Man. Immediately after the torment of those days, the sun will be darkened, and the moon will not shed light; stars will fall from the sky, and the heavenly bodies will be shaken.

"Now learn a parable of the fig tree: when the branches from the root of Jessie sprout forth and blossom leaves, you know summer is close by. When you see these events, know it is near, directly before the door. I say to you: This generation will not pass away until all I've told you has happened. Heaven and Earth will pass away, but my words will never pass away.

"No one knows what day or hour, not even the Son, nor do angels in Heaven, but only my Father. The coming of the Son of Man will be just like the days of Noah. They ate and drank and were given in marriage, whereupon Noah entered the ark knowing the flood would come to carry away all. So will be the coming of the Son of Man. Two men will be in a field; one will be taken, the other left behind. Therefore, you are to keep heavy watch, for you know not what day the Lord will come. If the master of a house knew when a thief would come, he would be prepared to safeguard his valuables. So too, be prepared, for the Son of Man will come when you least expect.

"When the Son of Man comes from the clouds on high, he will sit on his throne with heavenly glory. He will address the nations to separate the sheep from the goats. Then their king will say to his sheep, 'Come, you who are blessed of God, enter the kingdom of life everlasting, for I was hungry, and you gave me something to eat. I was thirsty, and you gave me water; I was homeless, and you sheltered me; I was distraught, and you comforted me.'"

"Then the righteous will answer him, 'Lord, when did we see you hungry and feed you, or thirsty and gave you something to drink? When did we see you homeless to house you? When did we see you sick and in prison and visit you?'

"The king will reply, 'If you have done it to the least of my followers, you have done it for me.'

"Then he will say to the goats, 'Depart from me, you who made yourselves accursed, into the hollows of darkness, which has been prepared for the devil and his minions.'

"All shall receive their wages, some to eternal happiness, and some to damnation."

CHAPTER 11

Jesus gathered seventy-two believers to send ahead two by two into every town. They questioned him, "What do we tell others when they say to us, 'By what authority does this Jesus forgive sins? Only the Lord Jehovah can forgive sins.'"

He taught them, "If I am to become a king by the hand of God Himself, then I am to have a kingdom. A king must be ruler of his domain; for such reason is a crown given. I shall govern over both Jews and Gentiles and all the angels in Heaven. Are you not the king of your home? Do you not say who will enter and who will not? Are you not able to look away from the wrongdoings of your guests if you so choose, permitting some but not others? Amen, my kingdom shall be my home. I shall forgive whom I choose; those I accept will come and live as guests in my home."

They further questioned him. "What will you forgive, Master? Who will the king allow into his home?"

"I say to you, who will you ask into your home? Would you seek someone who did not believe in you? Would you want someone who had no respect for you? Someone who felt you had no authority and should not be counted on as a ruler? Would you select someone who would not listen to your wishes and decrees?"

All agreed, "No, we would not want such a person."

"Those who receive me, who will live by my decrees and follow my wishes, are the chosen who shall come into my kingdom and will feast at my table. They shall dance and sing, for I shall wipe the tears from their eyes. I will be the king over my people. The blessed shall come without money and still prosper. Nor shall know grief, sorrow, or the ravages of death, for my Father shall raise them from their grave to live with me forever."

"How about the rest?" they asked. "What about those who refuse you?"

"Do you not send away those who reject you? I also have the same right to send them away. As you would allow them to travel to another home, I cannot send them away to another realm, as there will be no realm to send them to. They must be burnt up in a raging fire as discarded chaff. Know I have told you beforehand.

"I send you out to announce that the kingdom of Heaven is at hand. This is what you will say. You will tell them they who receive me shall not be disappointed; they who receive me shall live forever, for I will take them by the hand to everlasting promise. Let they who scorn continue to scorn, and the scoffers to scoff. I offer what I offer."

The seventy-two left him to preach the gospel in surrounding towns and synagogues, acquiring many brethren who began to preach of him.

The mother of Zebedee's sons, James and John, came to Jesus with her sons and asked, "Allow my sons to sit on your left and right in your kingdom."

He answered, "It is not up to me who will sit on my left and right. These places belong to those for whom they have been prepared by my Father."

Jesus again appeared at the temple courts a few days later to teach and heal. The scribes and Pharisees brought a woman who was one of them to Jesus and contrived a story about her to test him.

"This woman was caught in the act of adultery. The law of Moses said we are to stone her. What say you?"

Jesus used his finger and wrote in the ground "lie" for his disciples to read. He threw a stone before the woman.

"Let him who is among you without sin cast the first stone."

The men turned and left. Jesus asked her, "Is there no one to condemn you?"

"No one, sir," she said.

"Then neither do I condemn you. Go your way and lie no more."

His disciples laughed at her as she left.

Thereafter, he spoke to the crowds and temple elders without parables. "I am the light of the world. Whoever chooses to follow me will never walk in darkness but will have the eternal light of life."

The Pharisees challenged, "How valid can your words be for you to appear as your own witness?"

He answered, "In your law, it is written that the testimony of two men will be valid. I testify in my behalf; my other witness is my Father, the Lord God, who has sent me. The words I speak are those His prophet has told me to speak, and I know he is true in sending me to you because he speaks for God and has no reason to lie. He is with me even now." Jesus pointed to the prophet, who was sitting away from the crowd. "You are of this world while I belong to another. I told you that you will die in your sins if you do not believe I am the one I claim to be. You truly will die in your sins."

The temple priests had heard of a blind man being healed and sent for him to receive his testimony. After asking him to explain how it happened, he said, "The one called Jesus put some mud on my eyes and told me to wash it off in the pool. As I washed, my eyes were opened to see."

They asked, "Is this man a prophet?"

Fearful of saying yes or no, he answered, "Whether or not he is a prophet, I do not know. I only know once I was blind, but now I see."

The priests did not wholly believe he was blind, so they sent for his parents to support his claim. "Is this your son whom you say was born blind? Why is he able to see?"

"Yes, he is our son," they said, "and he was born blind. How he can see, we do not know. Ask him yourself, for he is of age."

They said that from fear of being put out of the temple and refrained from acknowledging Jesus as a Christ. So again, the healed man was asked, "We already know this Jesus as a great sinful man. Speak truthfully. How could he have opened your eyes?"

He said, "If he is a sinner, I do not know or care. All I can say is, I was blind, but now I see."

Again they insisted on knowing, "By what method did he evoke your sight?"

"Are you interested because you want to become his followers? I have already told you once. Isn't that enough? Everyone knows God does not hear sinners, yet should they become God-fearing and do His will, He will hear and oblige. Perhaps this Jesus was such a person."

They were angry and said, "You were born entirely in sin, and you think you can teach us?" That day, they put him out of the temple.

Jesus heard they had put him out, and when he came across him again, he asked, "Do you believe in the Son of Man?"

"Are you one of the same?"

"Yes," Jesus said, "even as I stand before you now."

The man fell to his knees, saying, "Lord, I believe you are God's Anointed."

Jesus said to him, "For judgment I have come into this world so that those who do not see may see, and those who see may become blind."

Some members of the Pharisees overheard him and interrupted, "Are we blind as well?"

"If you were blind," Jesus said, "you would have no sin; but since you say, 'We can see,' your sins remain.

"Verily, verily, I say to you, they who do not enter through the front door to join the flock of sheep, but climb in some other way, are thieves and robbers. Those who enter openly by the door become shepherds of the flock. The gatekeeper will readily open the door, and the sheep will know his voice. He calls his sheep by name and leads them out. Truly, I say to you, I am the door of the sheep. If anyone enters through me, they shall be saved and will go in and out, finding good pasture. The thief comes only to plunder; I come to prepare them for their freedom and redemption so that they might someday have life and have it abundantly. I am the good shepherd; the good shepherd lays down his life for his sheep. I know my own, and my own know me. For this reason, my

Father loves me because I have decided to lay down my life so that it may be taken up again. No one takes my life from me, but I lay it down of my free will."

People began arguing when they heard him and said, "He has a demon and has gone insane."

Others defended him by saying, "These are not the teachings of a devil, nor can a devil open the eyes of a blind man."

At the time of winter, Jesus appeared at the portico of Solomon. The sons of Israel, those who had previously heard him speak, said, "Why do you speak so many riddles? If you are a Messiah, just come out and say so boldly."

"I have already told you who I am, but you have not believed. It is not for you to believe because you are not my sheep. My sheep would hear my voice and follow me to eternal life, where they will never perish or be taken from me. My Father, your God, has given me His children, and no one has more power than He that they could steal them from His hand. Know also that God and I have become joined through His spirit."

Becoming angered, the people gathered stones to throw at him. In his defense, Jesus asked, "Which of the good works I have shown you do you stone me for performing?"

"You know it is not for any good work that we stone you. We know what kind of life you have lived, and now you claim to be joined with our holy God."

Jesus said, "How can you cry, 'Blasphemy,' because I said I am the adopted Son of God? Can God adopt, forgive, and sanctify anyone He chooses?"

Becoming impatient, they stoned him further and chased him with clubs through the streets and alleyways, shouting curses. Finding a safe place to hide, he could escape the mob as they passed by without noticing. Leaving there, he departed to a place beyond the Jordan where John had baptized.

Now a certain man called Lazarus of Bethany was ill and went to be with his fathers. His sisters, Mary and Martha, had sent word to Jesus that the one he loved had died. Hearing this, he lingered two days longer. Then he said to his disciples, "Let us return to Judea." Trying to protect him, they pleaded with him to change his mind. "Rabbi, the people were seeking to stone you, and now you want to return to them?"

He explained, "Our friend, Lazarus, has died for the glory of God." When they arrived, they found many friends consoling Mary and Martha as they were still mourning. Martha, seeing Jesus arrive, approached him, saying, "O Lord, if you had only been here, my brother would not have died."

Jesus comforted her, saying, "Your brother shall rise from the grave."

Though she was still in tears, she acknowledged him, saying, "This I already know; he will rise on the last day in the resurrection of the dead."

Jesus said, "I am the resurrection and the life; they who receive me shall live even if they die, and anyone who lives and receives me shall never die. Do you believe this, Martha?"

"Yes, Lord, I believe you to be a Messiah expected to come into the world."

"Get your sister Mary and your brethren so that we may go to the tomb."

They all proceeded to the burial site, a cave with a huge stone set against the opening. "Remove the stone," Jesus said.

Martha refused his request, saying, "Lord, there will be a stench, for he has been dead for four days."

"Did I not explain you will see the glory of God?" So the stone was taken away.

Jesus looked up to Heaven to pray. "Father in Heaven, I know you are with me always and have brought me here to display your glory. I pray to make your power known so all will know you have sent me." After he prayed these words, he approached the cave, shouting, "Lazarus, come forth!"

The crowd watched as Lazarus came from the cave, bound hand and foot with wrappings. They tended to him and brought him back home while others remained behind to honor Jesus as a Christ. When friends of the Pharisees saw them bowing before Jesus, they ran to the synagogue to tell what they saw.

News of the resurrection spread quickly, causing excitement even among his disciples, who never realized how much God would do for His Son. So they followed him with zeal.

Six days before Passover, Jesus and his disciples came to Bethany and were dining with Lazarus. Martha and Mary both served and tended to the table. After they ate, Mary anointed Jesus' feet with expensive perfume and then dried his feet with her hair.

One of Jesus' disciples, Judas Iscariot, became upset with her doing this and chastised her, for he was concerned and mindful of the poor. "Why was the perfume not sold for its value and the money given to the poor?"

Jesus saw need to defend her, saying, "Leave her be, for she is preparing me for burial. The poor she will always have to tend, but she will not always have me to tend."

Many people had heard Jesus was dining with Lazarus and came out to see them, particularly Lazarus. Because of him, many people ceased listening to the priests and began to believe in Jesus.

The day thereafter, those who had seen Jesus raise Lazarus from his tomb heard Jesus was coming into Jerusalem. They took palm branches and horns out to greet him, shouting, "Hosanna to the Highest, blessed is he who comes in the name of the Lord."

The prophet went to Jesus and said, "Have one of your followers go and fetch a colt, a foal of an ass, for you to ride on so that what was prophesied will come true: 'Have no fear, daughter of Zion, a king shall come; he has been humbled, even seated on a donkey's colt.'"

"What if I refuse to ride it? Haven't I had enough shame?" Jesus said, becoming rebellious.

"'I will chastise him with the rod of men and the strokes of the sons of men,'" said the prophet. "God knows how to remove pride from the depths of a man."

"You have not answered my question. What if I refuse?"

The prophet answered, "I think you already know the answer."

When the colt was brought forth, everyone stood around Jesus, wondering why he had asked for such a lowly foal. He lowered himself on its back and could not raise his head for shame as they led him into the city before crowds of laughing people. His feet staggered on the ground as he tried to balance himself on the colt that could not support his weight. The rejoicing of the few only caused him to scowl. Those who laughed threw fruit at him as they would at a clown.

The Pharisees watched from afar, and said to the high priest, "The city is going after him and believing, and what is the synagogue doing to stop it?"

When it was over, Jesus walked away alone down an empty side street. He listened to the laughter and jeers of the crowd behind him, who continued to call after him, refusing to stop their snickering. They held palm branches over their heads, shouting, "Look, I am a king!" The weight of his shame and humiliation caused him to stay in solitude.

CHAPTER 12

From the day of his entry on a colt into Jerusalem, Jesus taught his disciples his hour to be glorified was soon to come. He told them he must stay in Jerusalem to suffer many hardships at the hands of the temple elders, scribes, and chief priests, and that they must kill him and be raised from the grave after three days.

On hearing this, Peter said, "This will never happen to you, for I will not permit it!"

Jesus stepped away from him, saying, "Get behind me, Satan; you are offensive to me!"

Some men had approached, pretending to be his followers, but they had been sent by the synagogue's elders to keep watch on him, hoping to find some evidence of wrongdoing. They said, "Is it right according to God's ways to pay taxes to Caesar?"

Seeing their dishonesty, he said, "Whose face is on a denarius?"

"Caesar's," they answered.

"Then give to Caesar that which belongs to Caesar. Give to God that which belongs to God."

Determined to return with evidence of wrongdoing, they questioned further, "Moses' law states a man must marry his dead brother's wife and have children for his brother. If there happened to be seven brothers and the first married a woman and died childless, then the second through the seventh each married her and died, leaving no children, whose wife will she be at the resurrection?"

"Know I have told you, those chosen to celebrate at the resurrection shall not marry but will be given like angels."

They dared not ask any more questions but continued to follow as if they were believers.

Jesus then went to the poor, barren, and lost, saying, "I am a true vine, and my Father is the vinedresser. All those who branch from me and do not bear fruit, He shall take away; every branch that bears fruit, He shall nurture to bear more fruit. Therefore, abide in me that you flourish richly, for a branch cannot bring abundance unless it abides in a strong vine. As my Father chose to love me, a great sinner, I have loved you. I give to you freely so you may abide in my love today, tomorrow, and forever. These teachings I tell you so that your joy will be made full and your burden light. This is my commandment: that you love one another. Greater love no man has than one who lays down his life for another. Even the lowest among you is considered greater than I by my Father. If my Father were to find only one among you who was lower than me, He would not ask me for my life. No one invests their precious possessions for something less precious, but they would invest their precious belongings for something more precious. You are considered more precious to Him than His Son whom He loves. It is my Father's will that no one perish, but all be brought to repentance, even unto salvation. All that belongs to my Father belongs to me; all I own is yours. I give this to you freely, asking nothing in return except to love one another as I have loved you.

"Soon I am going to Him who sent me, and you will see me no more. It will be to your advantage I go so that my Father may send the Comforters who will testify of me. They will remind you of everything I have said to you. In them, my people will have comfort and safety. They will not speak on their own; they will speak only what they hear, tell you what is to come, and make the wonders of God known to you. Elijah will come to restore what needs to be restored.

"These blessings I have spoken to you, so you may be kept from stumbling. When my Father sends the other Advocate, he will come in the spirit of truth, gather up what is mine, and reveal many splendors to you. He shall come with a sword to afflict and condemn the world concerning sin, righteousness, and judgment.

He shall not command on his own, but whatever he hears from God, he will command and reveal to you."

Then Jesus said to the crowd and his disciples, "The scribes and Pharisees sit in the absence of Moses. You are to heed their words, yet do not copy their ways, for they preach but do not conform to their preaching. They will put heavy burdens on you to carry yet place none on themselves. Their good deeds are done for the praise of other men's eyes. They broaden their phylacteries, lengthen the tassels of their garments, and relish places of honor at banquets and the chief seats in synagogues. They stand in the marketplace to be greeted and called rabbis. You are my own; therefore, do not strive to be called rabbi, for you have only one teacher, which is I. Do not consider anyone on Earth, father, for your true Father is in Heaven. Do not strive to be called a leader, for you have only one leader, which is I. Whoever cares to exalt themselves shall be humbled; whoever cares to humble themselves shall be exalted.

"Woe be to you, scribes and Pharisees, for you direct the people away from Heaven's door because the door is not open to you.

"Woe be to you, hypocrites, for you devour widows' houses, easing your guilt with long prayers, yet you will still receive your punishment.

"Woe be to you, hypocrites, for you travel across the land and sea to make one proselyte, yet when found, you have him become as bad as you are.

"Woe be to you, blind guides, for who say, 'Swearing by the temple is nothing, but better it is to swear by the gold of the temple as an obligation.' Such fools and blind men you are. Which is more important, the gold or the temple that sanctified the gold? Then you say, 'It is nothing to swear by the altar, but meaningful to swear by the offering upon it.' I say to you, what is more important, the offering or the altar that sanctifies the offering? He who swears, swears by the altar and everything upon the altar. He who swears by the temple swears by it, and He who blesses the temple. He who swears by Heaven swears by the throne of God and by Him who is exalted upon the throne.

"Woe be to you, scribes and Pharisees, for you give a tenth of your spices but neglect the laws of justice, mercy, and faithfulness. You strain out a gnat but swallow a camel.

"Woe be to you, scribes and Pharisees, for the outside of you is polished clean, while the inside is full of greed and self-indulgence.

"Woe be to you, hypocrites, for you are like whitewashed tombs, beautiful on the outside, but inside you bear the bones of dead men.

"Woe be to you, scribes and Pharisees, for you build the tombs of the prophets and decorate the graves of the righteous, saying, 'If we had been living in the days of our fathers, we would not have shed the blood of prophets.' You bear witness against yourselves that you are the sons of those who killed the prophets. Brood of vipers, how can you escape the damnation of Hell?

"Therefore, you will be sent prophets and wise men; some you will kill, crucify, and persecute from city to city. Upon you, the guilt of all the shed blood of righteous men will fall."

CHAPTER 13

Then came the day of Unleavened Bread, on which the Passover lamb had to be sacrificed. Jesus sent some disciples into the city to prepare a place to eat the Passover. They made all the arrangements required for the holiday in an upper guest dining room.

The rest of his disciples had also been invited. Coming together, they went to the city; being guided by Jesus to the upper room, they walked up the winding staircase single file.

The prophet went to Judas Iscariot and, pulling him into the hallway, said, "Judas, when the Passover meal is finished, go to the temple and speak to the high priest. Tell him where Jesus can be found. We will be either here or at the Garden of Gethsemane."

Judas became startled and questioned him. "What is this you are telling me? The rabbis have nothing but contempt for Jesus. Do you want to see him get thrown in prison?"

"You must do as I say. It must be done so that the Scriptures can be fulfilled."

"They know I am a follower of Jesus, so why would they believe me? The priests would think it was some trap."

"Not if you tell them you are doing it for the money. They always pay out rewards for information they seek and would believe you are doing it for the money. Tell them the teachings of your childhood are stronger than his teachings, and your conscience does not allow him to continue preaching as he does. I know that is just what they want to hear."

"What of the soldiers? Wouldn't the high priest get the soldiers to arrest Jesus?"

"Yes, just as you say."

"If this must be done for the prophecies, why do you not go instead?"

"Because they would not believe me. You have been seen with him. As you have said, they know you are one of his followers, but I have been seen very little."

"Why not ask one of the others to go? Why does it have to be me?"

"Because they are not as learned as you and would not understand."

"If the prophecies say he will be delivered to his enemies, why does he not surrender himself to them? Is he not aware of what must be?"

"Yes, he is aware. It is not enough for him to deliver himself. The rabbis need someone to give witness against him. Without a witness from among the common people, all they can do is accuse. They cannot be both accuser and witness."

"What unlawful act am I to say I witnessed him doing? He has done no wrong against them."

"Tell them he speaks of being a king and tries to get people to follow his decrees."

"Isn't there anyone else to do this?"

"No, believe me, there isn't. I'm sure I understand all the others well enough to know they would not comprehend and certainly would not be convincing if they tried."

Judas paused momentarily, staring into the room at Jesus and the guests immersed in conversation. "Very well, if this must be done, I will do as you ask. What of the money? I certainly could not keep the silver."

"I don't care what you do with the money. Give it to the poor, if you will."

"All right, I'll do as you request," Judas agreed and re-entered, taking his place at the table.

They tasted the food and bitter herbs in respect to the law of Moses. Each lit a candle before him, joining in songs of praise to the Lord Almighty. It was a festive time when Hebrews, both young and old, put aside their worries of the present and fears of the future to give thanks for their deliverance from the bonds of Egypt. They did not know Jesus had brought them together to bid them farewell. The candles waxed low from the length of the evening. Jesus sat erect at his place, attracting their attention.

"My friends, now you see me, but in a short while, you will see me no more. I shall go to my Father's house to prepare a place for you. There is one among you who will be sent to betray me."

They were startled to hear such words and insisted on knowing, "Who is it who betrays you, Lord? We would never betray you," they said.

Jesus continued to say his farewell. "I know you would have me among you, but it is best I go to my Father, where I shall sit at His right hand to intercede for you. I have taught you to live in peace and love, forgiving your brother seven times seven. I send you out into the world to preach of my secret coming. Those with ears will hear; those with eyes will see, for I am the light of the world. A light is not kept hidden but is raised for all to see. Soon my Father shall glorify my name as I have glorified His. I will be a Savior to them who receive me; they who receive shall be saved on the day of judgment.

"If you love me, you will keep my commandments. Because I live, you will also live. On that day, you will realize I am a bridge to the Father. I am in my Father's heart. You are in my heart, and I am in your heart. My Father will love them who love me."

Then he took bread and gave thanks, saying, "Eat this bread; this is my body, that I give up for the sake of all mankind so that they may have their heavenly king."

His followers passed the bread from one to another; each broke off a piece to eat. Then Jesus took a pitcher of wine and, holding it up, again spoke, "Drink of this wine; this is my blood, that will be shed for the remission of my sins; then I shall be made pure and blameless in the eyes of the Lord. The world must have its earthly king, and I shall prepare the way for the kingdom of God to come upon Earth where all will live as one.

"God has said, 'I will put my laws in their minds and write them on their hearts.' This is so you will always live by my words. Then He said, 'I will remember their sins no more.' This new covenant you shall have, as God promised. My blood shall release the new and everlasting covenant."

They took the wine, each pouring a portion into their goblet.

Peter nudged the prophet and said, "Ask him who it is."

The prophet rebuked him, leaned on Jesus and whispered, "I have already prepared Judas to betray you."

Jesus had to pause, knowing he would be brought to his time of punishment, and thinking of Judas over himself, he said, "Woe to the person who is sent to betray me. It would be better for him never to have been born, as the dark side will work to make his life a misery, for he will enable the world to receive their king."

"Certainly, you do not mean me?" Judas said.

Jesus answered, "Yes, it is you. Go and do what you must do."

Judas' doubts about his assignment turned him to fear. He looked to the prophet to stand in defense of him, yet all he received was an encouraging nod.

Having no further way to stall and feeling the silence and cold stares from everyone at the table, Judas stood and left the room. Going out into the night, he headed directly to the high priest.

When dinner was over, the prophet took Jesus outside, leaving the rest to talk among themselves. While standing in private on the balcony, the prophet instructed him, "There is but one more chore for you to do before being taken to your time of punishment."

"Why do you say, 'One more chore'? I thought I had done everything you have told me."

"So has said the Lord God of Israel, "You are to wash the feet of your disciples on bended knee with a bowed head before man and God, and the dirt you remove will represent the stain of pride God is washing from your being."

"Am I expected to wash feet now? How much longer do you think I can bear up under all this? Now I am washing feet!"

"So has said the God of Israel."

"No! I won't do it! You wash feet if you want, but leave me out! I have lived as one under a curse; then I am paraded around the countryside to be spit at, stoned, laughed at, and humiliated on an ass' colt. I am left without family or friend, and now I am washing feet! No! I won't do it!" Jesus folded his arms and turned aside.

"We will wait for you," the prophet said, returning inside, leaving him alone.

For a time, he was hardly missed while they became more immersed in discussion, yet when he lingered, they questioned, "Where is Jesus? Did he leave without us?" He returned inside and, bringing water and cloth, went before them to wash their feet. When they refused to permit him, he said, "Unless I wash your feet, you can have no part of me, for I will no longer be your Messiah." So they permitted him. "There will come a time when you will understand why I do this," Jesus said. When he came to Peter, he said, "A person who has bathed has cleansed his body and needs only his feet washed, yet not all of you are clean." He said that knowing who would really betray him.

No one spoke but watched as he worked his way around the table. The washcloth splashed in the basin, so one could have realized what phase he was at with each person. When finished, he spoke sternly, "Do you see what I have done? If I am made to wash feet, so too must you, for students are not above their teacher." He threw down the washcloth. "Come, let us leave this place." He walked by them, unable to look into any of their faces, and was first out the door.

They went to the Mount of Olives, where Jesus addressed them, "Because of me, you have gathered here, and because of me you will all be scattered, for it is written, 'I will strike the shepherd, and his sheep will be scattered.'"

"Never will we leave you," Peter said.

"Peter, I see Satan is sifting you as wheat, yet I pray all your faith is not taken away that you may return to strengthen those who have not seen and heard what you have seen and heard."

Peter said, "Rabbi, even if all these fall away, I shall never fall away."

"I say to you," Jesus spoke almost absent-mindedly, "this night before the cock crows, you shall have denied me three times."

Peter said, "Even if I have to die with you, I will never deny you." All the disciples agreed with him.

Jesus gazed at the ground, amazed at the chain of events that brought him to see the completion of his ministry. "And he was numbered with the transgressors," he remarked to himself.

They followed him to the Garden of Gethsemane, where he said to his disciples, "Rest here while I go over and pray." He took Peter, James, and John and grieved with sorrow and fear. He told them, "I am distraught to the point of death; remain with me to help me pray." Moving further away, he collapsed on his face and prayed, for he was terrified of the cross and suffering such a death. Beads of sweat fell from his face as he desperately approached God in every way he had learned possible. He begged, pleaded, and groaned to be forgiven and spared the agony of crucifixion and the public shame before his enemies. Never was there a person to submit willingly to such public disgrace and humiliation.

An hour passed, and returning to his disciples, he found them sleeping. Having been wrought by his anxiety, Jesus kicked Peter and shouted, "Wake up! You say you are my follower? You can't even help me pray for one hour!"

Peter strained to open his eyes. "I'm sorry, Jesus. The spirit may be willing, but my flesh is tired."

Seeing the futility of further talk, Jesus turned away in disgust and returned to pray by himself.

He took long pauses to reflect on his life. The simplicity of his days and meager pleasure he enjoyed was recalled with longing as he sat remembering his former hopes and ambitions before being persuaded to assume his ministry. He was overwhelmed with sinful debts and had only one way to cleanse them.

He prayed, "My Father, my God, you have forgiven the heathen and those who bend the knee to Baal. You have pardoned the warrior who ravaged the fields of the defenseless and looked away from the scorching breath of those who deny and blaspheme you. Can there be no deliverance for me save to undergo such suffering? Grant me solace in your grace and relief from the burden I carry. I am the likeness of a sinful man in every way, coming before your throne to prostrate myself in front of your grandeur and infinite kindness. Am I that repugnant in your eyes that you cannot grant a measure of your generous mercy?"

He again went to his disciples, only to find they had returned to sleep. Feeling it senseless to awaken them, he moved to the open grove a third time to pray further. The evening brought forth a cold wind, yet no chill could be blamed for his trembling.

"My Father, my God, where can I go, or how long should I labor to win your favor and receive a pardon for my disbelief and wrongdoings? To what shall I liken my life? I am but a fledgling fallen from its nest that needs a gentle hand to restore me. I beg you, my Father, my God, to spare me this hour and let this cup pass, yet let not my will but your will be done."

When he had finished praying, he went to his disciples, who were sleeping. His attention was taken by a group of soldiers who marched toward him, along with some Pharisees carrying weapons and lanterns. Judas Iscariot was among them. The noise of their arrival awoke the disciples.

A homeless man, one of many, in the garden was taking a bath in a ditch. When he saw the soldiers arrive, he wrapped himself in a sheet and followed Jesus when Jesus went to meet the soldiers. The man became frightened and started to flee when one soldier approached him. The soldier grabbed the sheet, and the man ran away naked.

The soldiers came forth to seize and bind Jesus. Then Peter came forward, drew his sword, and struck the ear of a high priest's servant.

Jesus cried out, "No more of this! Do you think I cannot drink the cup my Father has given me?" He asked the soldiers, "Did I ever lead a rebellion that you came with swords and clubs to capture me? When I taught at the temple courts, you did not arrest me. Yet know, you do this because my Father has willed what the prophets spoke of might be fulfilled."

The disciples fled into the night after Peter had angered the soldiers by drawing his sword.

They took Jesus to the high priest, the elders, and teachers of the law. After they left with him, the prophet turned to Peter, saying, "Are you trying to keep him from receiving his kingdom?"

CHAPTER 14

The soldiers and those from the temple who had accompanied them brought Jesus directly through the temple gates and into a small room where he was guarded. The soldiers guarding him during the night used him to pass the time by blindfolding and assaulting his body, saying, "Prophesy to us, Messiah. Tell us who hit you?" They continued to slap and spit on him until the fun of it had worn off.

Now the prophet and Peter had followed behind at a distance. When they arrived at the temple, the prophet was allowed in, for the priests knew him. Peter remained outside the gate, warming himself. The prophet then gained permission to permit Peter inside and sent a girl messenger for him.

"Are you not one of this man's disciples?" the girl asked Peter.

"No, I'm not," he said.

A man who stood warming himself said, "Yes, you are one of his disciples. Your accent gives you away."

"No, I am not."

An aide of the high priest, a relative of the man whose ear Peter had cut, noticed him and spoke up, "Didn't I see you with the Nazarene at the grove? You were the one who struck with the sword."

Peter said, "I have already told you; I am not the one. I don't know him." He began to curse. "Go away! Leave me alone!"

He started to move away from them and then suddenly heard the crow of a rooster. Remembering the words of Jesus, he became afraid and ran away.

Come morning, Jesus was brought before the Sanhedrin that had quickly formed and had gathered many people to speak out against him. While many of their testimonies contradicted one another, none were approached to explain why. After hearing from each witness, they were still at a loss what charge they could bring against him. It was only then they brought him forth and allowed him to speak. The prophet was standing in the rear of the room.

"I have spoken openly to those before me. I always spoke to people with openness and never in secret. Why don't you ask those to whom I spoke? They would tell you if I had done wrong."

One official came forth and struck him in the face. "Is this the respect you show to the high priest?"

"If I said something wrong," Jesus said, "tell me what was wrong about it. If I spoke the truth, tell me what was wrong about it. If I spoke the truth, tell me why you cared to strike me."

The high priest asked, "Tell us, are you a Christ of the Most High God?"

"I have already told you, and you did not believe. Yes, I am a Christ and shall sit at the right hand of the Most High God to judge the living and the dead. As well, in the future, you will see the Son of Man, coming in the clouds of Heaven, who will sit beside a Mighty One."

"See how he blasphemes!" said the high priest. "Truly, we wait for the Lord's Anointed to regain the throne of David, but would God ever adopt such a Son as him? Everyone knows how he has lived his life." Turning back to Jesus, he asked, "Why do you say you are the adopted Son of God and have lived your life so ungodly?"

Jesus bowed his head in shame and gave no answer.

"Why should there be any more witnesses? We have heard enough. Is this man worthy of death or not?"

The entire assembly agreed with the high priest, so the temple priests and elders brought Jesus to the front of Pilate's palace. Pilate came forward asking, "What crime do you accuse him of committing?"

"If he were not a criminal, we wouldn't deliver him to you," they said. "He was found guilty of sorcery and blasphemy against the Most High God."

Pilate said, "What care do I have of your religion? Take him away and treat him according to your own law."

They insisted, "This man, Jesus, opposes payment of taxes to Caesar and claims to be a king. He works toward rebellion and to disrupt our nation." They ensured they made the charge publicly.

Pilate was forced to respond since he was dutifully bound to uphold the laws of Rome. Turning to an aide, he said, "If I look away from this charge that was pronounced publicly, I may be condemned by my superiors for not upholding my position. Yet what will his followers do if I decide to punish him? I was not sent here to stir an uprising. How would that look to my superiors?"

"The man is Galilean," his aide said. "That is Herod's territory. Why not send him to Herod?"

Pilate returned to the outside of the palace to address them. "Why do you bring him to me? If he is Galilean, send him to Herod."

Messengers from the priests went before them to inform Herod they were coming with Jesus, the one who called himself a Christ. Herod was there to greet the soldiers and priests, for he was eager to meet the one called Jesus, hoping to see him perform a miracle. When he questioned him about his miracles, Jesus did not answer but allowed the elders to accuse him.

"What fakery is this that you will not perform a miracle for me?" Herod said, and began mocking him in front of all to see. His aides placed a large rag over Jesus' shoulders for a robe to ridicule him, saying, "This will help you feel more like a king." Then they bowed before him, slapping and abusing him. When they were through using him for amusement, he was sent back to Pilate.

Pilate became overly cautious when he saw them return with Jesus. He assembled the priests, elders, and the crowd that gathered into one place called the Stone Pavement and brought Jesus before them. Pilate sat in the judgment seat in front of Jesus. He quieted the crowd and spoke to them. "You brought me this man, claiming he was an enemy of the state, yet I have examined him and found no wrongful doing, nor has Herod, for he has sent this man back to me. Whereas he has done nothing to deserve death, I will have him punished and then released."

The crowd became more unsettled and demanded his death, saying, "He has blasphemed our God and is a practitioner of sorcery!"

Pilate turned to Jesus and said, "Do you have anything to say in your defense? Don't you realize I have the power to free you or put you to death?"

Jesus said, "You have such power only because my Father gave it to you."

Pilate feared him, for Jesus spoke confidently and not as a sorcerer. Wanting to release him, Pilate asked, "Are you a king?"

"I am, yet my kingdom is not of this world."

When the priests heard him speak, they interrupted with more accusations.

"What have you to say about this?"

Jesus had no reply and stayed silent.

It had become the governor's custom to release a prisoner the people chose when they celebrated Passover. Pilate believed he could use the custom as an excuse to release Jesus, for he knew the priests convicted him out of envy. Pilate said to the crowd, "Because it is the Passover feast, I will only punish him and release him to you as is the custom."

The crowd shouted back, "Give us Barabbas instead!"

Now Barabbas had taken part in a rebellion and was a murderer. Pilate ignored them and turned away, sending Jesus out to be flogged.

Determined to have fun, the soldiers pulled his beard, punched, and spit on him.

Enraged by their abuse, Jesus lunged at them, knocking two soldiers to the ground and thrust another against a wall. He was about to smash him with his fists when he noticed the prophet standing alone behind the gate. The prophet stood motionless, quietly staring at him through the gate's bars. Seeing him, Jesus relaxed his stance, loosened his grip on the soldier, letting him go and allowing them to abuse him.

They hit him all the harder and tied a clump of thorn branches down on his head for a crown. They laughed, "Hail the king of the Jews," in all mockery. All the while, Jesus stood numb, watching the prophet stare at him from across the way. Then they laid him over a bench and flogged him. When he collapsed into a faint, they revived him by dashing a bucket of water into his face.

Once again, Pilate went before the crowd, believing their tempers had settled. "Behold the man," Pilate said, pointing to Jesus, still covered with a rag and a clump of thorns. I return him to you. I have no reason to punish him further."

The crowd shouted back, "Give us Barabbas! We want Barabbas!"

"Which of the two do you want me to release, this Jesus, who has done no wrong against you, or Barabbas, who is guilty of murder?"

"Barabbas!" they all agreed.

"What then shall be done with the one called Christ who claims to be your king?"

"Crucify him! Crucify him!"

"What crime has he committed?" Pilate asked.

"We have no king but Caesar. Let Caesar be our king!" They shouted all the louder.

Pilate saw he was getting nowhere and was afraid of the uproar that had started. He took water and washed his hands. As was the custom, he took a board and wrote the charge against him, 'Jesus—King of the Jews.' He dried his hands, saying, "I am innocent of this man's blood. Let his blood be on you." He handed Jesus over to be crucified and had Barabbas released from prison.

CHAPTER 15

The soldiers took charge of Jesus and two other men from prison who were scheduled to die that day. Jesus fell beneath his cross, leading them through the city as he had been severely beaten. Having been whipped to his feet, he fell again and again. A man named Simon, who had just entered the city from Cyrene, watched the procession of men carrying their crosses and the crowd of mourners who followed behind weeping. Seeing him standing there, the soldiers made him help Jesus take his cross to a place called Golgotha.

They disrobed him, except for his undergarment, and divided his clothes among them. They nailed and tied him to the cross, then raised it with ropes and allowed the cross to fall into the ground, standing upright. The two other men were crucified to his left and right. One of the men said to Jesus, "If you are a Christ, save yourself and us as well." The other criminal silenced him by saying, "Why do you complain? We are guilty and deserve our punishment. This man has done no wrong against the state." Turning his head to Jesus, he said, "Jesus, remember me in your kingdom."

Jesus said, "I tell you, this day you will be with me in paradise."

Mary, his mother, heard of the crucifixion and came to Golgotha. Jesus looked down and saw the prophet standing beside her and said, "Mother, behold your son; son, behold your mother." From that day onward, the prophet cared for Mary until she died.

The crowd who had cried out for his death and the priests gathered before him to remind him of his shame. They hurled insults and threw stones and dirt, saying, "He claims to be the

Son of the Almighty; let's see if he can save himself." They laughed at him with such unity it seemed as if the whole world had assembled before him to expend a lifetime of laughter. He groaned in agony and cried out in pain. His screams only aroused the people to mimic him in mockery. He pleaded and cried in his final hour, saying, "I thirst." Some soldiers heard him and, using a long pole, placed a sponge soaked in wine vinegar to his lips in all spite. He then cried out, "My God, my God, why did I ever forsake you?" When people saw him speaking, they said, "Look, he calls for Elijah to come save him," believing it was good for another laugh. At the ninth hour, he breathed his last and died.

The next day was to be a Sabbath, and the priests went to Pilate, asking for the legs of those crucified to be broken so that their bodies could be taken down. Soldiers came and broke the legs of the first man and then the other, but coming to Jesus, they found he was already dead, and rather than break his legs, the soldier pierced Jesus' side with a spear that brought forth a flow of blood. The prophet watched from across the way, for he had lingered behind when the crowd had dispersed so he could help remove Jesus from the cross.

As evening approached, Joseph of Arimathea, an esteemed temple member, became distraught over what he had seen and went boldly to Pilate, asking for the body of Jesus. He had believed in Jesus, yet fear of ridicule forced him to believe in secret. The centurion had just told Pilate that Jesus and the other two men had died, so Pilate, seeing no harm, allowed him to take the body.

Joseph and Nicodemus took the body and prepared it for burial, using strips of linen, myrrh, and ointments, as was Jewish custom. They placed the body in Joseph's newly made tomb, carved from rock in a garden close to Golgotha. Having rolled a large stone slab across its opening, they left.

The following day, the priests and Pharisees went before Pilate and said, "We remember when that deceiver was alive, he told people, 'In three days I will rise.' Therefore, allow the grave to be made secure so that his disciples cannot come to steal him away and then claim he has risen from the dead, for the last deception will be worse than the first.

Pilate agreed. "You have soldiers assigned to you. Go and have your will."

So they made the tomb as secure as possible with guards to sit all day and night. They then placed a seal on the stone.

That evening, Judas Iscariot, distraught over what he had seen and heard, sought the prophet. He was troubled and said, "Why did Jesus say, 'The dark side will make my life a misery'? All I did was what you had instructed. If there is anyone's life to be made a misery by the dark side, it's yours. If it were not for you guiding and instructing Jesus, he would never have completed his task in life."

"Certain events in life must be accomplished by those chosen to accomplish them. I, myself, am not exempt from the dark side's retaliation. They have already made my life a misery, which was something I was expecting. I always knew demon attacks would come; they have certainly come against me in more ways than one. Still, we are blessed that the Lord God has anointed us with the great honor of serving Him."

"What honor is this that I have become responsible for killing the Son of the Most High God? The devil even made me watch Jesus carry his cross. My soul is racked with guilt that I cannot even eat."

"Do not be troubled over what has happened, and do not listen to any guilt about you, for the guilt is not yours."

"If you knew they would harm him, why did you send me to get the soldiers?"

"It was to make what was said of him come true, 'I will correct him with the rod of men and the strokes of the sons of men, but My lovingkindness shall not depart from him ... and his throne and his kingdom will endure before Me forever.' Without the shedding of his blood, his sins cannot be forgiven. Christ's task was to convince mankind who he was, though his reputation as someone of the world was ever dominant. As Isaiah had written, 'He bore the sins of many.' Many are a group of people. If you took all the sins a group of people are guilty of, he was guilty of them all and had only one way to cleanse them. Whereas Jesus could not convince creation that God had sent a Messiah, he was punished for not fulfilling his assignment; had Jesus lived a pious life, many would have accepted his ministry and teaching. Refusing to believe the gospel, their sin of disbelief was on him. The sins of the many caused him to die, and the stone the builders rejected became the cornerstone. By his stripes, we are healed of our spirit. If mankind had never sinned, there would be no need for a Messiah, yet man did indeed fall away, causing God to send a Deliverer. He suffered because of the sins of creation and came to know the grief man's iniquity has caused. Jesus was sent to precede the Seed of the Woman and to herald the Son of Joseph. He came to work the beginning of salvation for man's eternal soul. As it was foretold, he fell into sin himself and had to be chastised to be made pure and blameless in the eyes of God. He was brought to learn obedience through his suffering. Rejoice, you opened the final door that enabled the judge to receive his power that will condemn the devil and his legions to their just reward. When the Son of Joseph arrives to smite the earth with every plague, judgment shall come, and the kingdom will be established."

Judas did not rejoice in his accomplishment; he departed, looking very troubled.

CHAPTER 16

Early on the first day of the week, the rabbis who had accused Jesus before Pilate and the same ones who had a seal placed on the tomb's entrance went to the tomb to ensure that Jesus was still dead, for they feared him. After inspecting the seal, they said to the guards, "Slide the stone away so that we may see his rotting corpse, and then everyone will know what a liar he was."

The soldiers broke the seal and rolled away the stone. When they did, they saw Jesus standing on the other side, looking at them. He came out from the tomb and walked away from their presence. They told no one what they saw.

Later that morning, Mary of Magdala, from whom Jesus had cast out devils, greeted the prophet and Peter. She was running from the direction of the burial garden and excitedly called to them, "They have taken the Lord out of the tomb, and no one knows where they have placed him!"

After hearing her, they immediately left and ran toward the tomb. The prophet outran Peter and arrived there first. He bent down to peer inside. Then Peter came and entered the tomb. The prophet followed him in, and seeing the discarded linen strips and cloth, he said, "He has risen! He has risen!" He immediately left to tell the others, leaving Peter alone inside the tomb.

Mary returned to the garden and cried on the ground near a pool. She heard a man behind her, saying, "Woman, why are you weeping?"

She did not care to turn around but answered while looking at his reflection in the pool. "They have taken my Lord from his tomb." She spoke as if he were the gardener. "Sir, if you have carried him away, tell me where he was placed so I may find him."

Jesus called to her, "Mary."

She turned to see him and cried out, "Rabbi!" She went to hold on to him to pay him reverence.

"Go to my brethren and tell them what you have seen, for I will soon return to my Father and God, to your Father and God."

So she went into the city to his brothers, sisters, mother, and disciples, crying happily and shouting, "He has risen, the Lord Jesus has risen!"

When the prophet returned home, he found Jesus waiting there for him, and they embraced each other and wept.

When evening came, the disciples met behind locked doors in fear of the priests and people of the city. They heard a knock at the door, and when they opened it, they saw Jesus standing there in the flesh. They all rushed to the door to greet him and were all amazed he knew where to find them.

Jesus said to them, "As my Father has sent me, so will I send you. I pray my Father will breathe His holy spirit on you." They then ate and talked the evening through.

A week later, they again met behind locked doors. Jesus came to them in the flesh to speak more. There was another among them called Thomas, who had not been around in the early days. He had told the disciples, "Unless I see the nail imprints in his hands and feet have disappeared, I will not believe." Jesus said to Thomas, "Place your finger here in my hand and here in my side and no longer doubt but believe."

Thomas then said, "I have lived to see my Messiah!"

"Because you have seen, you believe," Jesus said. "Blessed are they who did not see, yet believe."

Again Jesus came to them, this time at the Sea of Tiberias. Some disciples had been fishing and, not having caught anything, were returning to shore. Jesus was on the beach and called to them, "What fish have you caught today?" They did not recognize him at first and answered, "None."

"Cast your net on the right side of the boat, for there are fish for you."

Believing he had seen a school of fish near the surface, they cast their net, and when they tried to haul it in, found the net too heavy with fish to bring in all the catch. The prophet was aboard the boat and said, "Look, it's Jesus!" When they arrived on shore, a fire was already prepared, having fish and bread on it.

Jesus said, "Bring up some of the fish in your net." They sat around the fire to eat and talk. When they were finished, Jesus asked Peter, "Peter, do you love me more than these?"

"Yes, Lord, you know I do."

Jesus asked, "Why haven't you fed my sheep?"

Peter had no answer and remained silent.

"And you say you love me?"

Peter replied, "But of course I do."

Jesus questioned, "Why haven't you tended to my flock?"

Again Peter had no answer.

"And you say you love me?"

"Of course I do," Peter said. "Why do you ask me three times?"

"Why have you led them astray?"

Again Peter did not answer.

"Truly I say to you," Jesus said, "when you were younger, you would dress yourself and go wherever you wished; yet when you grow old, someone else will dress you and bring you where you do not want to go."

Then Jesus said, "Let us be gone from here." So they followed.

Then Peter turned and saw the prophet following behind, as he was prone to do. He sought Jesus' attention and asked, "What about that man? I heard you say something to him regarding your second coming."

Jesus answered, "If I want one like him to be alive when I return, what is that to you?"

Because he said those words, a rumor spread among the followers that the prophet would not die. Though Jesus did not say that he would not die, he only wanted one like him to be alive at his second coming.

They went among the people openly, in fear of no one, healing and preaching such that a large crowd gathered around them. Many people were brought to believe, having seen and heard him. Moving to the vicinity of Bethany, Jesus walked up a hill before a crowd of people who had heard of his resurrection and came running out to see. A child ran up to him, and he picked her up to carry her. The prophet stood at the base of the hill and smiled as he watched Jesus standing before the crowd and waved goodbye to him. People knelt as he walked before them, and they sang "Hosanna in the Highest" and other songs of praise and glory. Jesus wept as he passed by them, for all that was prophesied about him had come true. It was overwhelming to him to realize he had come to his last day on Earth. He touched the children who lined the way to bless them; he had come to love one and all. His disciples walked behind him as he climbed higher so all could see.

He addressed the crowd, "Go into all the nations, even to the world, and preach the gospel to every soul. Wherever two or more are gathered in my name, there my Father shall be, even to the ends of the earth."

The people waited for him to say more, yet as they did, a cloud of light surrounded him, raising him above their heads, where he dissolved into the light, leaving only the blue sky before them.

CHAPTER 17

Shortly after the ascension, the prophet sent for the disciples to meet at his home to remind them of their assignments and to gain their written testimony. He said to them, "We must be careful to record for history's sake, as well as for believers in all nations, the teachings of Jesus and his instructions. To remind you of his many deeds and words, I have written them for you in bits and pieces. I will give each of you a copy to arrange in whatever order you best remember and then write your testimony to what you have witnessed. When you are finished, we can make copies and distribute them to the brethren so that they may be accurate in their teachings. I have already composed my testimony."

They began glancing over the package of parchments they were to take with them.

"You should stay as close as possible to the events and proceedings I noted since they are the most significant. As you will agree, we cannot write everything that happened in his ministry."

They left his home, taking with them the parchments where the events concerning the passing of Jesus were recorded, and each began to compose his testimony of what he had witnessed. They preached extensively, having been filled with spirit and acquired many of their brethren as believers who also helped spread the gospel of Jesus the Christ.

The prophet preached extensively, inviting people into his home to lecture on who and what Jesus was and to ensure their hope in Jesus would not be in vain. In a short while, the followers of Jesus grew to where they were forced to assemble in an open field. The prophet taught them, "To accept the gift of salvation and receive the spirit of the Lord God, pray, 'Forgive my sins, O Lord God, and allow me to come into your kingdom. Thank you for allowing me to accept your Son as my Lord and Savior. Grant me the gift of your saving grace so that I may be raised to live with you forever. Come into my heart and heal me of my spirit so I may have the salvation of my soul.'"

To those in faith in Christ who were yet unclaimed, he said, "Stand on the redemptive promise of the Son of Joseph, who is to come. I pray you may be ready when the day of redemption is proclaimed.

"Every unredeemed body can be a dwelling for the devil, and as you would fight to maintain your home, so too will they. Affix your faith and belief on the promised redemption. To recognize and give loyalty to the Son of Joseph and his earthly kingdom before he even appears is the same as believing in him after he appears. When you pray, say, 'Blessed be the name of the Lord God, who shall send His Son to redeem our bodies from sickness and infirmity. Grant me the gift of redemption that will be secured in his holy work and hasten his coming to bring your righteousness and kingdom to Earth.' You shall live long and fruitful as the days of a tree, being nourished by the grace of God.

"Know it shall come to pass at the end of the age, salvation in its fullest will be revealed in all splendor, and the world will realize God knows all truths."

The gospel of Jesus Christ spread throughout the land to every kindred and tongue. It was taken to Jews and Gentiles, to lands across the sea. Saints of God grew in vast numbers as belief in His word strengthened under persecution and suffering. Their trials helped to reaffirm the sincerity of their hope. No longer did they feel distant from their Creator. People of faith began to wait for the blessed day the kingdom would come on Earth with all its promises and eternal glory. Amen.

End